Railway World SPECIAL

# THE WEST HIGHLAND LINES

## NEIL CAPLAN

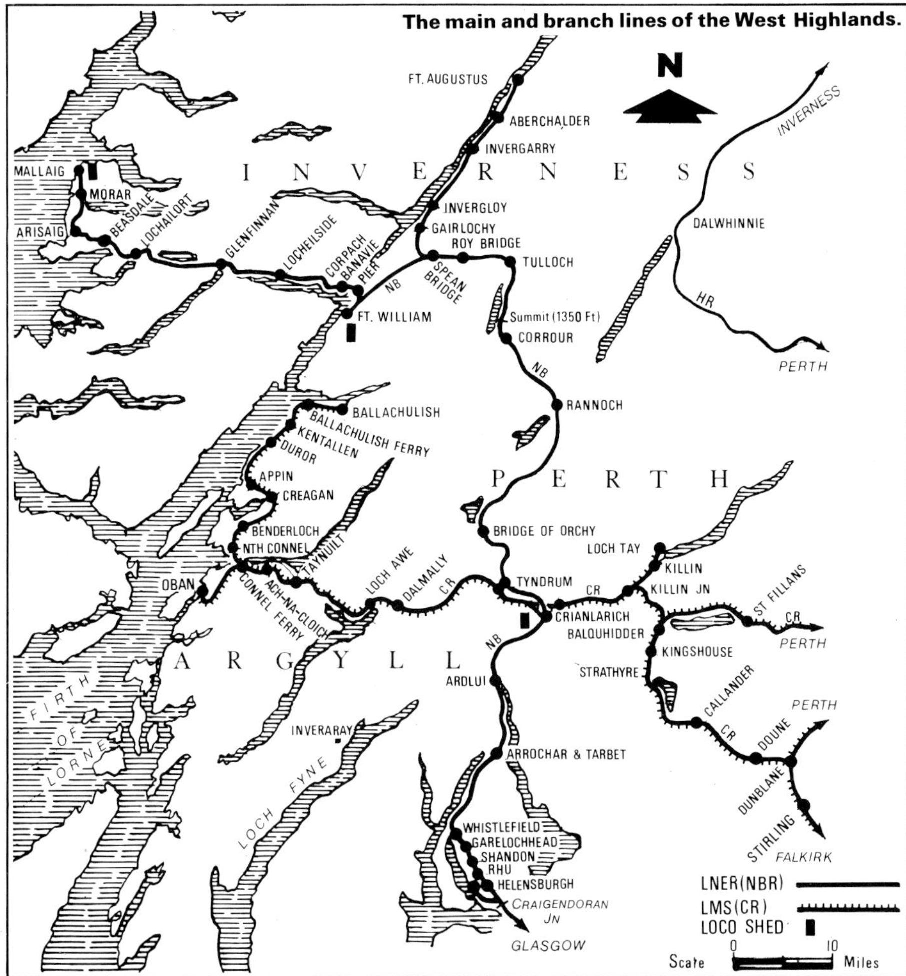


Contents



*Front cover:*
**BR Standard '5' 4-6-0 No 73109 makes a vigorous departure from Fort William with 6.50am Mallaig-Glasgow on 27 May 1961.** *M. Mensing*

*Back cover, top:*
**Stanier 'Black Five' 4-6-0 No 44798 pulls into Callander station with a train from Oban in July 1958.** *The late W. Oliver/Colour-Rail (SC137)*

*Back cover, bottom:*
**BRCW Type 2 (later Class 27) Bo-Bo diesel-electric No D5348 heads an afternoon Glasgow Queen St-Mallaig working alongside Loch Treig on 16 July 1965.** *M. Mensing/Colour-Rail (DE251)*

*Left:*
**By the shore of Loch Awe. Stanier '5' 4-6-0 No 45016 heads a down freight which includes oil tankers for the Oban fuel depots in August 1961.** *S. C. Crook*

First published 1988
Second impression 1990

ISBN 0 7110 1766 2

Published by
IAN ALLAN LTD
Coombelands House Weybridge KT15 1HY
Telephone: Weybridge (0932) 858511
Printed by Ian Allan Printing at their works at Coombelands in Runnymede, England

# Preface

Historically, *the* West Highland Line between Craigendoran Junction by the Clyde and Mallaig on the West Coast was entirely distinct from the Callander & Oban Line. The former line of 140 miles was opened to Fort William in 1894 and to Mallaig in 1901; the latter line of 71 miles was opened to Oban in 1880. The two lines have become one operationally since the closure in 1965 of the Callander & Oban Line between Crianlarich and Callander. The Oban trains use the West Highland Line's route as far as the spur connection at Crianlarich (Upper).

Both lines have been railways of great character and both remain routes of much scenic interest. The Oban Line was diminished in every way by the loss of its eastern section, but even as built it fell far short of the railway interest and scenic glory of the West Highland Line proper. It is the latter which therefore has pride of place here. Indeed, the West Highland Line has a fascination in its natural setting, and in the historical and romantic associations of that setting, which have never been fully matched by any other railway in Great Britain.

The Waverley Route over the 98 miles between Edinburgh and Carlisle once rivalled the West Highland Line in some respects, but it was much shorter and scenically less dramatic. The Waverley is now a lost railway — it was closed entirely in 1969 (I have paid tribute to this great line in *The Waverley Route*, Ian Allan, 1985). The most northerly of the railways of the West Highlands happily remains intact and certainly the 'Kyle Line' has something of the quality of the West Highland but it is less than half the length of the latter and its setting lacks the full grandeur and the romantic associations of the West Highland, though it is only fair to add that even in the 1980s the Kyle Line has been too often undervalued.

Across the Border, there is no line which can be compared realistically with the West Highland Line. I have known well and admired greatly the Settle to Carlisle route and I recognise that its principal engineering structures are on a greater scale than those of the West Highland. But the 'mountain' section of the Settle to Carlisle Line is so short compared with almost the entire course of the West Highland and it has nothing to be compared with the lochs and coastal scenery of the latter. Nor does its setting rival Lochaber's rich historical and romantic associations. Today the Settle to Carlisle Line has less of railway operational interest than the vigorous West Highland Line — a sad reflection when one recalls the long era of the St Pancras route in Anglo-Scottish travel.

A slender book like this allows space for only a terse summary of the historical background to the West Highland Lines. There are, however, several sources for those who wish for more of the history. For the West Highland Line proper, there is the late John Thomas's *The West Highland Railway* (David & Charles, 1965) and the late George Dow's *The Story of the West Highland* (LNER 1944). For the Oban Line, there is the succinct account by Oswald S. Nock in *The Caledonian Railway* (Ian Allan, 1962) and Nock has written also about both lines in other books, including *Scottish Railways* (Nelson, 1948). The recent past and the near-contemporary scene have been so well covered by Colin Boocock in *British Rail At Work: ScotRail* (Ian Allan, 1986).

*Right:*
**A setting which is so typically West Highland — the line by the water's edge, the mountainside and the sweeping curve of the track. This mixed train of coaches and vans is also typical of the Mallaig Extension Line down the years. A 'K1' 2-6-0 heads the 13.00 Mallaig-Glasgow in April 1961.** *G. F. Heiron*

Here, the focus is very much on the lines as they were during the long era of steam — as working railways and as routes set in glorious countryside. John Thomas wrote of the line he so loved: 'The West Highland Line is above all else a scenic railway and photographs, to do it justice, must illustrate its scenic attractions' and this applies also to the Oban Line. But the scenic attractions should not be allowed to obscure the consideration that the two lines have been a vital part of the transport system of the West Highlands, serving its people and their industry and commerce, including the highly important tourist industry. Operationally, these lines have been in most respects as challenging as any in Great Britain and this remains true of the West Highland Line even in the diesel age.

Happily, during the past 30 years or so a goòd many photographers have captured brilliantly both the intrinsic railway interest and the scenic glories of the lines. It is a pity that the photographic record of the 1920s and the 1930s is so much more restricted but these lines have been remote for most photographers. Although the steam locomotive is dominant here, the diesels are very far from being left out of the picture — they appear more often than one might expect, given the far longer era of steam operation. The explanation is that railway photographers since the 1960s have used the natural setting to offset the so-limited range of motive power and the absence of smoke and steam as picture-makers. This will be evident particularly in Chapter 2 describing the course and construction of the lines.

I have not lost sight — in a haze of nostalgia for the steam locomotive — of the crucial fact that the West Highland Lines are alive and well today. Despite the economic difficulties of the 1970s and 1980s, there have been some encouraging developments on the West Highland Lines, as elsewhere on the enterprising ScotRail system. This applies particularly to freight traffic over the West Highland — the traffic that is absolutely essential for the survival of such a long railway running through sparsely-populated and difficult terrain. The striking new technology of Radio

*Left:*
**The snow-capped mountains and the snow-plough fitted to the locomotive are reminders that severe winter conditions were often part of the challenge of working the Callander & Oban Line. Stanier '5' 4-6-0 No 45178 climbs from Killin Junction to Glen Ogle with the 12.05 Oban-Glasgow in March 1955.**
*W. J. V. Anderson*

*Below:*
**The motive power had changed but the superb scenery remained as it had been in 1901 when the West Highland at last reached the coast at Mallaig. Class 27 No 27001 approaches Lochailort with the Mallaig coaches of the overnight train from Euston on 15 February 1979.**
*Brian Morrison*

*Top right:*
**The pleasant setting of the Callander & Oban Line near Strathyre (part of the stretch closed in 1965). Stanier '5' 4-6-0 No 45396 is in charge of a Glasgow-Oban train, including coaches from Edinburgh, on 3 July 1957.** *David A. Anderson*

*Centre right:*
**Not as dramatic a setting as many along the West Highland Line but still a grand sweep of countryside near Roy Bridge. Class 27 No 27043 heads the 14.05 Mallaig-Glasgow on 27 May 1976.**
*Brian Morrison*

*Bottom right:*
**As the finest scenic route in Britain, the West Highland Line deserved to have the benefit of the 'Beaver-tail' Observation Cars which had been built for the streamlined 'Coronation' train in 1937. After being stored during the war, the cars were modified at Cowlairs. They gave long and excellent service on the line. One of them is seen being turned at Mallaig shed in September 1963.** *Author*

Electronic Token Block signalling (RETB) and train control is going forward swiftly with its promise of important cost reductions. For the steam railway enthusiasts, there is the bonus of ScotRail's scheduled summer steam workings on the Mallaig section and the charter steam workings of the prestigious 'Royal Scotsman' train from Glasgow — workings which have done so much to encourage more people to travel over the lines.

The West Highland Lines are *not* preservation set-pieces but rather working railways of continuing great importance to the economy of the area. The challenge of operating them can be experienced. Their fine engineering structures are intact. The superb natural setting has been little-touched by the years and the historical and romantic associations are as compelling as ever. The West Highland Lines have every right to claim the interest and active support of railway enthusiasts and of all people who have come under the spell of the West Highlands.

**Acknowledgements**
It may seem unfair in the eyes of authors but most railway books are judged at least as much by the illustrations as by the main text. This makes me all the more grateful to the many photographers who have contributed prints. A considerable proportion of these have not been published previously — an important point when the railway magazines are regularly publishing so many fine photographs of the current scene on the West Highland Lines. Mr Oswald Nock has been generous in allowing me to use his logs and other published material. Kaye Kettlewood and Stuart Sellar have helped me greatly as friends, but with the benefit also of their experience in ScotRail. It is no formality to mention the friendly interest and good advice of Michael Harris and Simon Forty of Ian Allan Ltd.

*Neil Caplan,*
*Cuckfield,*
*West Sussex*

# THE WEST HIGHLAND LINES

## CHAPTER 1

# The Railway Companies

A significant element in British railway history concerns the host of lines projected but never built. Many of these were of doubtful practicability and others, had they been built, would have proved disastrous financially. All this applied to the rugged and thinly-populated Scottish Highlands with schemes for lines to reach their furthest corners. Even when, in the 1860s, work first began on lines striking westwards from the Caledonian and Highland Railways, there was inadequate recognition of the engineering problems involved and of the huge costs likely to be borne.

The Callander & Oban Railway Company was formed to construct a line between the Caledonian Railway's system and the West Coast at Oban. Although Oban had been served by steamers giving a journey time to Glasgow of about 10hr, there was strong pressure for a railway which would give a much shorter journey time and a more frequent service. The Authorisation Bill was introduced in 1865 and it met with remarkably little opposition. From the outset the Callander & Oban Railway Company was effectively a vassal of the Caledonian Railway which both subscribed to the costs of building the line and undertook to work the new railway. The Caledonian was set on preventing the North British Railway from reaching the West Coast from Glasgow and its hold over the Callander & Oban was part of this strategy (it was in 1865-66 that the North British outflanked the Caledonian's grip on Glasgow itself by absorbing the Edinburgh & Glasgow Railway).

The course planned for the Oban Line was not at all an easy one with the severe climb up through Glen Ogle and the difficult terrain of the Pass of Brander by Ben Cruachan. The promoters had underestimated the task and it took 5 years for the railway to reach Glenoglehead — only 17 miles from Callander. The company's resources were exhausted and further work on the line had to be suspended (the railhead was given the name Killin though it was some miles from the village — it later became Killin Junction). The Caledonian worked this 17 mile stretch. The Callander & Oban Railway was forced by lack of money to obtain Parliamentary authorisation in 1870 to abandon the line beyond Tyndrum. Work then began westwards from Killin and it took another 3 years to cover the 15 miles to Tyndrum. In 1874 the Caledonian Railway injected more money into the Callander & Oban Railway to permit construction between Tyndrum and Oban and the coast was finally attained in 1880. The Callander & Oban became a subsidiary company of the Caledonian (unlike the West Highland Railway which was absorbed into the North British). The branch lines associated with the Oban Line are considered in Chapter 7.

Turning to the West Highland Railway Company, one finds a more complicated story. It probably was just as well for the building of a railway between the Clyde and the North West Coast that the task was not put in hand until the end of the 1880s. The experience of the Caledonian over the Oban Line was not lost on the North British Railway and it was decidedly cautious about becoming heavily involved in projects to build a railway to Fort William and beyond. The turning point came in 1882 with the launching of the project for the Glasgow & North Western Railway and the introduction of its Authorisation Bill. The planned course of this line was from the North British at a junction by Craigendoran up past Loch Lomond (on its eastern shore), through Glen Falloch and on to Glen Orchy. From

*Below:*
**Railways and steamers worked closely together in the development of tourism in the West Highlands and both the Caledonian and North British Railways owned large fleets. *Waverley* was built in 1899 for the North British and she later had a special association with the West Highland Line when passengers on the 1930s 'Northern Belle' train cruise enjoyed a trip aboard her from Craigendoran Pier. She is seen here in 1936, four years before she was sunk off Dunkirk.** *BR/LNER*

*Right:*
**The first locomotives in regular use over the Callander & Oban Line were from the 0-4-2 'Heavy Minerals' class built by Neilsens in 1871 for the Caledonian Railway.** *Ian Allan Library*

there, the line was to be taken into Glencoe and by Loch Leven and Loch Linnhe to Fort William, with a final section through the Great Glen to Inverness.

This ambitious project alarmed the Caledonian and Highland Railways who were allies in the existing mainline between Glasgow and Inverness via Perth. They bitterly opposed the Bill and it failed to pass despite a last-minute offer by the promoters to drop the proposal for the section between Fort William and Inverness. In the event, however, this did not prove too lengthy a setback and the hearings on the Bill had helped to widen understanding of the great need of the West Highlands for improved land transport links. The West Highland Railway Company was formed in 1889 and its Bill was introduced. The planned course from Craigendoran to Glen Orchy was similar to that of the 1882 project except that the line was to be taken up the western shore of Loch Lomond. From Bridge of Orchy, the line was to run across Rannoch Moor to Loch Treig and Tulloch before turning westwards to Spean Bridge and Fort William. The final section was to reach the coast at Roshven on the southern shore of Lochailort.

As on so many other occasions in Eastern Scotland and across the Border, the North British was now pursuing its own interests behind the façade of a nominally independent company. But the credibility of the West Highland Railway, and its only hope of financial viability, rested on the involvement of the North British. This was on a substantial scale: £150,000 towards the costs of construction and a 3½% return guaranteed to the stockholders of the West Highland Railway Company. The North British also agreed to work the railway with its own locomotives and rolling stock.

*Below:*
**An evocative scene at the original station at Fort William in 1914. A pair of the then new 'Glen' class 4-4-0s are seen leaving with the 17.05 sleeping car train for Glasgow and King's Cross — No 256 *Glen Douglas* was the pilot engine (now preserved).** *Crown Copyright/ National Railway Museum Collection (1112/82)*

The Caledonian and Highland Railways opposed the Bill even though it did not include a link with Inverness. By 1889, however, there was strong support for a railway to serve Lochaber and their opposition was ineffective. The larger difficulty in Parliament arose from the hostility of a few large landowners to the extension of the railway to Lochailort and the promoters found it prudent to drop this part of the Bill which then passed. But it was to take 12 years in all before the railway was built through to the coast. It was vital for the economy of Lochaber, as well as for the West Highland Railway and the North British, that the line should be extended to the coast. Only then could the railway benefit from the fishing industry and the Hebridean traffic, including tourism.

The first goal was to reach Fort William and this was attained with the opening of the line on 7 August 1894. By then Parliament had approved the West Highland Railway (Mallaig Extension) Act which authorised the construction of the railway from Fort William, Mallaig Junction, to the coast at Mallaig — the Admiralty's strong preference for a terminus and harbour at Mallaig had caused the dropping of the original plan for a terminus at Roshven. There remained the difficult hurdle of obtaining Government financial backing for the Mallaig Extension Line and the North British was insistent that such help must be given. It was not until 1896 that Parliament approved a Treasury Guarantee for a portion of the stock involved and a substantial grant of £30,000 towards the cost of the harbour at Mallaig.

*Above:*
**The Connel Ferry-Ballachulish branch was a notably fine scenic route in its own right and its closure in 1965 was a sad loss. In the glorious setting alongside Loch Leven, McIntosh '439' class 0-4-4T No 55224 is seen with a train for Oban in August 1961.** *S. C. Crook*

The Mallaig Extension Line was opened at last on 1 April 1901. Soon afterwards, the nominal role of the West Highland Railway Company was underlined with the North British being authorised in 1902 to replace the West Highland's stock by an issue of its own stock. The fiction of a separate company was ended in 1908 when the North British absorbed the West Highland Railway Company. This was a landmark indeed for the North British Railway — the company which had begun in southeast Scotland was established firmly on the northwest coast.

Centenaries are very much a part of British railway history and it is worth emphasising that the West Highland Line is still a good way short of attaining its centenary — that is, if completion through to Mallaig is taken as the base date. But there is a powerful case for regarding the completion of the 100 miles between Craigendoran Junction and Fort William in 1894 as the relevant year and therefore for celebrating the West Highland Line's centenary in 1994. Happily, the prospects of the West Highland Line reaching '100 up' are now far better than they seemed even in the 1970s. The Oban Line, of course, is well past its centenary, albeit as a shortened route since 1965.

*Left:*
**Over 1,300ft up and the snow fences and the additional cab protection for the crew tell their own story of the exposed course of the West Highland Line by Corrour Summit. LNER 'J36' 0-6-0 No 5237 with a down ballast train, c1930 (the snow fences are now derelict).** *Ian Allan Library*

# THE WEST HIGHLAND LINES

## CHAPTER 2

# The Course and Construction of the Lines

## The Oban Line

The Oban Line is mentioned first because it was built long before the West Highland Line. It was quite an ambitious project and certainly much more so than the promoters themselves had realised. Though it was relatively short — only 71 miles between Callander and Oban — even a glance at a contoured map of the ground to be covered by it reveals the challenge of such a mountainous region. The course of the Oban Line must seem somewhat roundabout with its northwards direction from Callander to Killin Junction, but the only alternative would have been to strike westwards along the loch shores into Glen Falloch and this course would have entailed heavy earthworks and tunnelling.

The advantage of the northerly course from Callander was that, once over the stiff climb at 1 in 50 through the Pass of Leny, there was a fairly level stretch alongside Loch Lubnaig and through Strathyre towards the western end of Loch Earn. The next section up through Glen Ogle to Glen Dochart was indeed hard going with a ruling gradient of 1 in 60 for some 7 miles. As already noted, this section in particular involved costly engineering works. The course along Glen Dochart and Strathfillan was not particularly difficult, but construction was slow and when Tyndrum was reached in 1873 it had taken eight years to build just 34 miles of railway. This exciting stretch of line is part of railway history with closure of the Callander & Oban east of Crianlarich (Lower) and it is difficult now to grasp how stern a challenge it presented

*Above left:*
**The first engineering structures of interest after leaving Callander were viaducts: This is the short but graceful crossing of the River Leny close to Callander. Stanier '5' 4-6-0 No 45357 with a down ballast train on 27 May 1957.** *W. A. C. Smith*

*Left:*
**The strongly built viaduct in the Pass of Leny. The working was the 'School Train' from Callander to Killin in September 1959, headed by No 57246 — a veteran survivor of the Caledonian 0-6-0 'Standard Goods' class.** *W. J. V. Anderson*

**Gradient profile — Dunblane to Oban.**

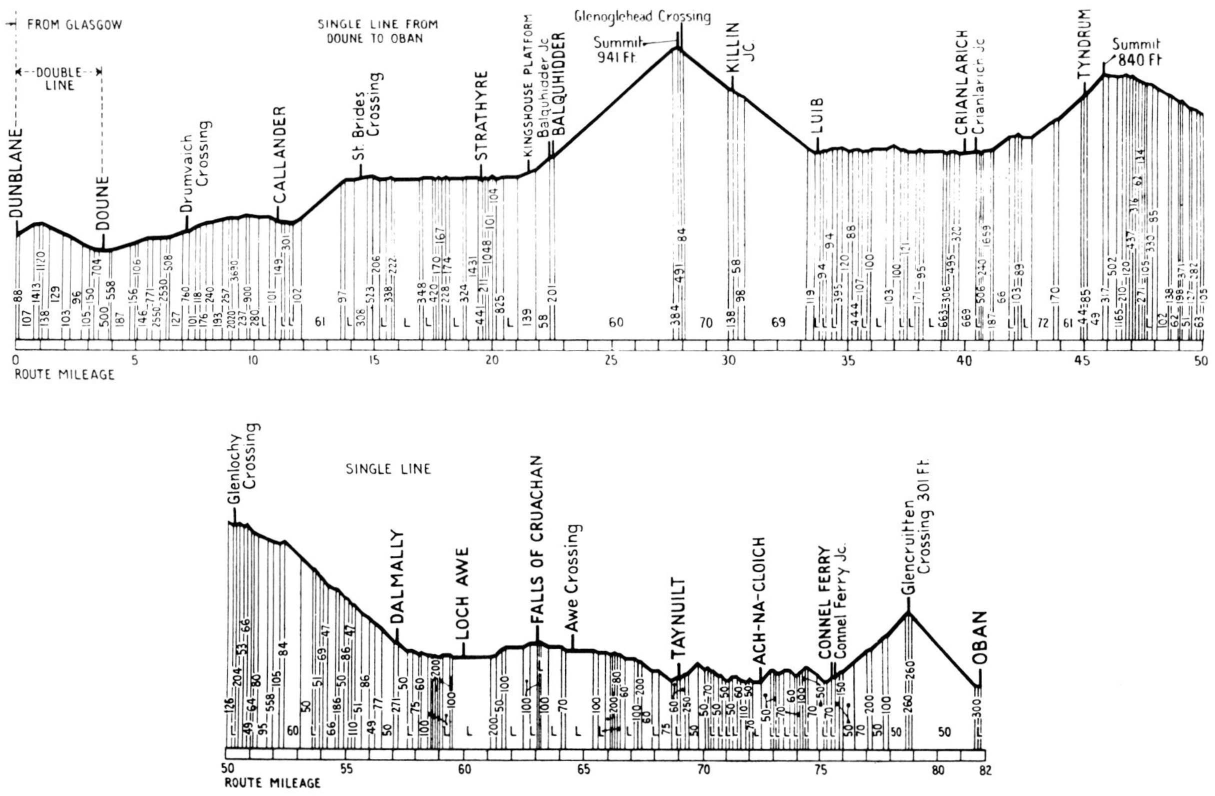

in steam days to locomotives hauling heavy trains up Glen Ogle to Killin Junction. This was not as dramatic a section as that westwards between Loch Awe and Loch Etive but there were lovely views across to Loch Earn, and Glen Ogle had rugged beauty.

Beyond Tyndrum, the Oban Line follows the course of the River Lochy to Dalmally — with towering Ben Lui to the south. This is falling ground on the down journey but for the up journey it involves several miles of hard going at 1 in 55 up to Glenlochy. After Dalmally, the Oban Line enters on its most exciting section as it swings southwards by Loch Awe before turning sharply into the western arm of Loch Awe. The narrow gorge of the River Awe on one side and the great mass of many-peaked Ben Cruachan on the other made construction extremely difficult. To negotiate the defile of the Pass of Brander, the line had to be carried well up the flank of the mountain on a narrow shelf. There were problems over landslides and these remained a continuing threat — special tripwire-actuated semaphore signals were installed as a warning for drivers in the event of a rock slide. These 10 miles of line provide a thrilling experience with the River Awe gorge and the waterfalls (nowadays one thinks of the great power station set within the mass of Ben Cruachan).

From Bridge of Awe, the course presented less difficulty but the outcropping of the rock of the coastal wall was a problem which entailed some short stretches of quite sharp grades — the most severe being the 1 in 50 by Glencruitten before the line swings round for the final descent to the shore at Oban. This explains why trains setting out from Oban in steam days were often double-headed as far as Connel Ferry. These 37 miles of railway from Tyndrum to Oban took 7 years to build. The Callander & Oban Line as built was a great scenic route and what remains still is notably good, even though it cannot be compared with the glory of the West Highland Line proper. In some ways, however, today's traveller over the Oban Line has the best of both worlds because there is the lovely stretch of the West Highland Line as far as Crianlarich and then the splendid run over the original Oban Line from Tyndrum to Oban.

*Below:*
**The Oban Line in Glen Ogle, with another School train headed by BR Standard '4' 2-6-4T No 80093 bound for Killin from Callander in June 1963.** *W. J. V. Anderson*

*Left:*
**Threading Glen Ogle on the hard climb to Killin Junction — Stanier '5' 4-6-0 No 45084 with a down freight in 1959.**
*W. J. V. Anderson*

*Below left:*
**The wintry scene in January 1980 at Crianlarich. Class 27 No 27003 with the 12.55 Glasgow-Oban was about to regain the Callander & Oban track from the spur connection with the West Highland Line at Crianlarich Upper. The original course of the Oban Line eastwards is seen on the left (it ends now in the siding at Crianlarich Lower used for loading timber).**
*Brian Morrison*

*Below:*
**The Pass of Brander alongside Ben Cruachan was the only possible course for the Oban Line but it was a difficult stretch to build. It is seen here in mellow summer mood in August 1961. A pair of Stanier '5' 4-6-0s with No 45443 leading, head an Oban-Glasgow train.** *S. C. Crook*

*Above:*
**A lovely setting of the Oban Line by the shore of Loch Etive on the approach to Connel Ferry. The train was a 'Television Excursion' to Oban on 24 May 1960, double-headed by Standard '5' 4-6-0s Nos 73108 and 73072.** *M. Mensing*

*Left:*
**The start of the stern climb up from the sea at Oban. The 12.25 Oban-Glasgow is hauled by Class 27 Bo-Bos Nos 27003 and 27010 on 27 September 1977. The pilot engine came off at Taynuilt — in steam days, a pilot was usually provided to assist the train engine as far as Connel Ferry.**
*G. A. Watt*

*Below:*
**Loch Awe signalbox in June 1961 — with one of the most beautiful settings of all boxes with the views over the long loch. In the background are the pier siding and jib crane which were used when a steamer service was operated down Loch Awe.**
*Author*

## The West Highland Line

This account of the course and construction of the West Highland Line is much fuller than the above account of the Oban Line. This is apt because the West Highland is 140 miles long and because the first 60 miles of the Oban route as it is today are over the southern course of the West Highland Line proper.

With such a progression of steep gradients, pronounced curvature of the track and heavy engineering works, the course of the West Highland must seem anything but ideal. However, the topography of the region is such that any realistic alternative course would have suffered from similar handicaps. The projected course of the 1882 Glasgow & North Western Railway was more direct with its approach to Fort William via Glencoe and the shore of Loch Linnhe, but such a course would have involved a difficult and costly traverse flanking the Black Mount and the construction of a major viaduct across Loch Leven.

The route gradient profile is included here and this itself tells us so much about the extremely difficult terrain — above all, the extended climb up to Corrour Summit from the south and, in the up direction, the 28-mile climb out of Fort William to Corrour at an average of 1 in 110. It shows also the special challenge of working the Mallaig Extension Line where the extended climbs over the Fort William section are replaced by so many short 'banks' pitched at 1 in 50. What the gradient profile itself cannot reveal is that the West Highland Line is tortuous in the extreme.

After the initial climb from Craigendoran Junction past Helensburgh Upper, the gradient eases briefly to Garelochhead but then stiffens to 1 in 55 with a longer stretch at 1 in 80 up to the line's first summit of 564ft at Glen Douglas. The next few miles on to Ardlui have very sharp curvature. Running through Glen Falloch the ruling grade to Crianlarich is sharp at 1 in 60. Across Strathfillan, there is the tough climb at 1 in 60/65 past Tyndrum Upper to the summit of 1,024ft at County March. There is then the short 'breather' of the descent to Bridge of Orchy before the climbing starts again up to Gorton. From Gorton to Rannoch the course is undulating but the restart from Rannoch station is stiff with 1½ miles at 1 in 53 before the final climb to the line's summit of 1,350ft at Corrour. This summit is only 134ft less than Britain's highest remaining summit worked by adhesion — the 1,484ft at Druimuachdar on the 'Highland' main-line (it is worth stating here that Corrour Summit was always given as 1,347ft but the ScotRail summit board now claims 1,350ft). The descent from Corrour is almost continuous but the course throughout is sinuous and limits the scope for fast downhill running — it was only over the final stretch by Mallaig Junction that speeds of 55-60mph were likely to be attained in steam days.

The Mallaig Extension Line is so different from the Fort William section because it does not involve any prolonged climbing. Instead, once the first 10 miles to Locheilside have been run almost on the level, there is the succession of short banks pitched at 1 in 50. The most demanding climb is that out of Glenfinnan. The swinging curves of the Mallaig section are also a big challenge, particularly over the

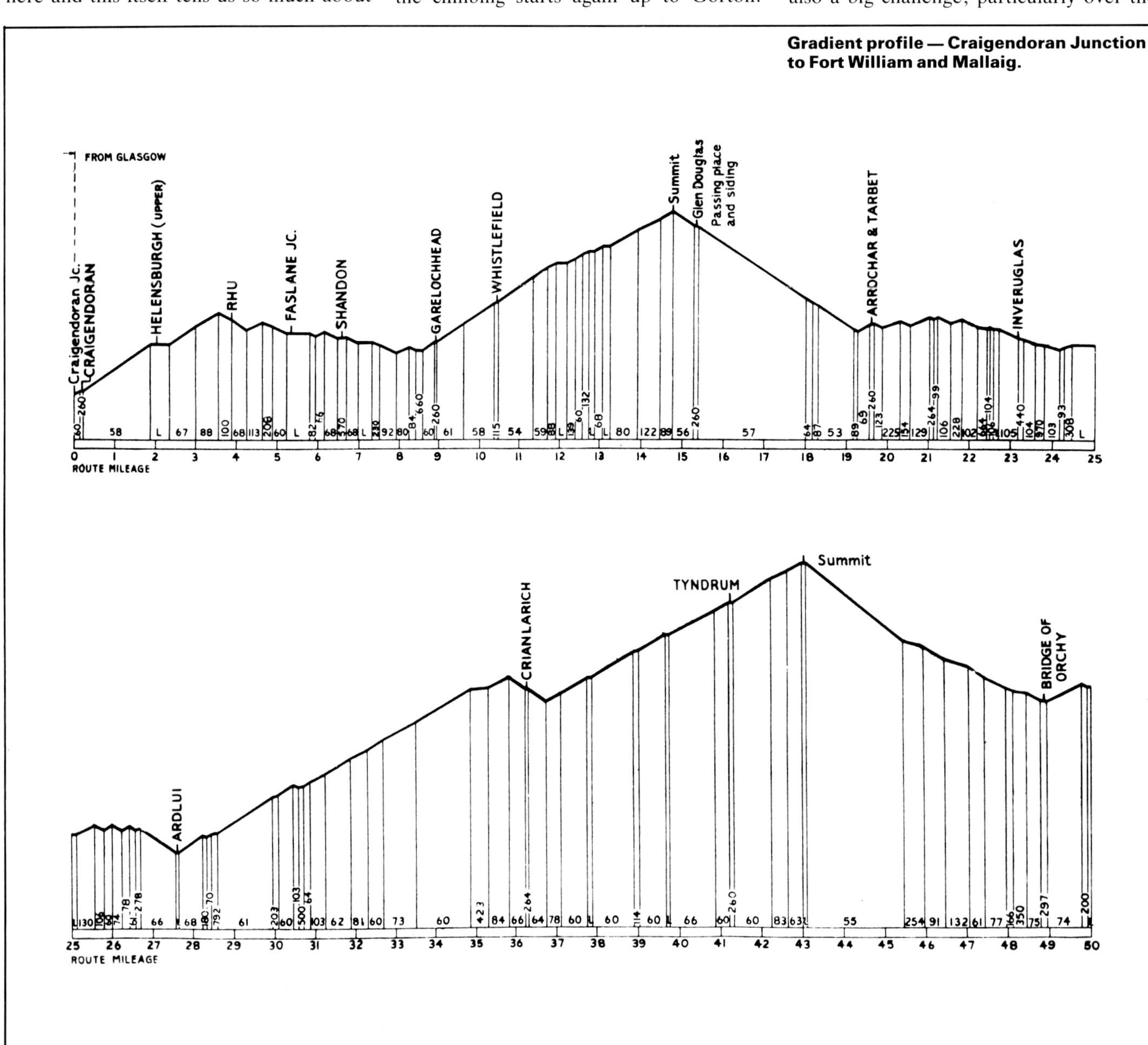

**Gradient profile — Craigendoran Junction to Fort William and Mallaig.**

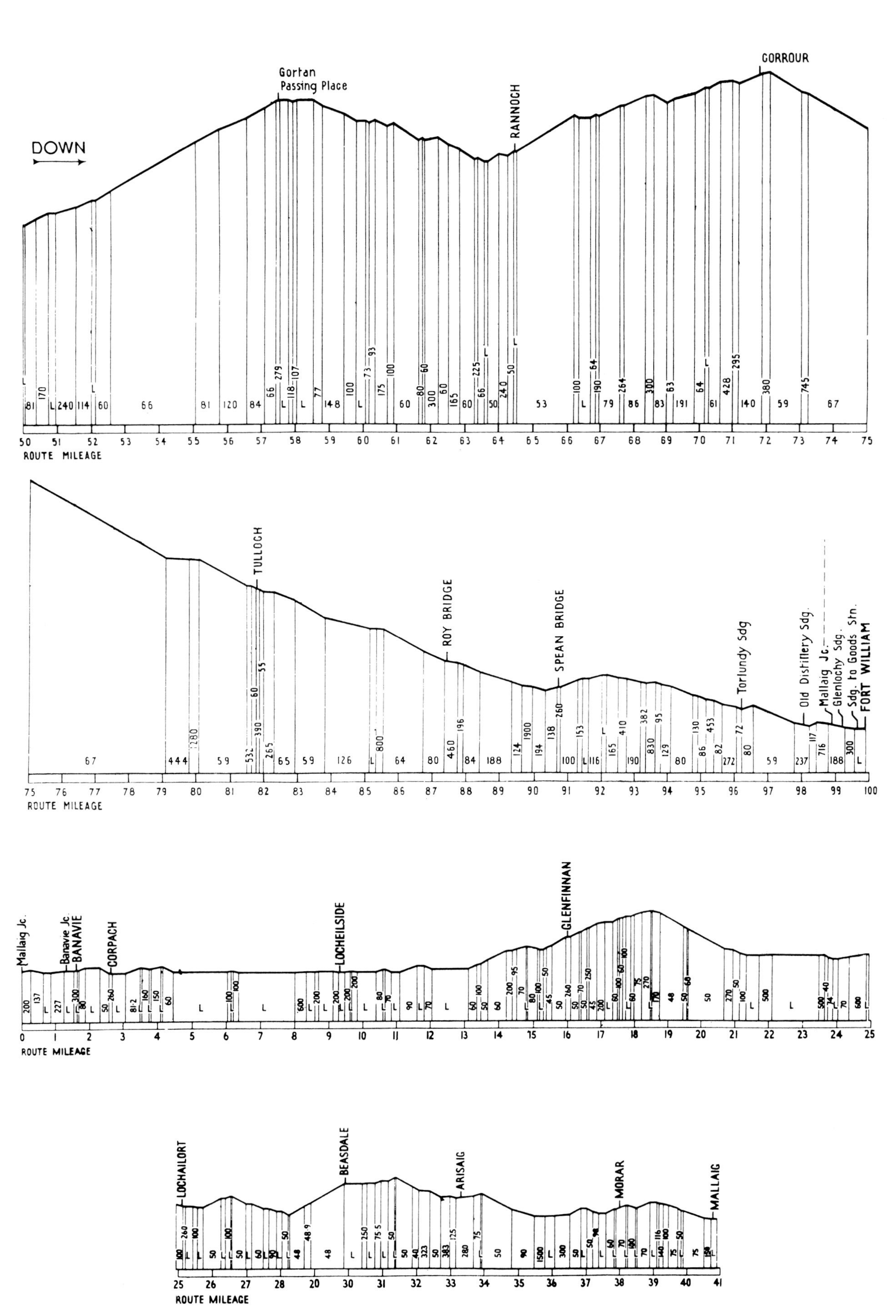
DOWN
Gortan Passing Place
RANNOCH
CORROUR
ROUTE MILEAGE
TULLOCH
ROY BRIDGE
SPEAN BRIDGE
Torlundy Sdg
Old Distillery Sdg.
Mallaig Jc.
Glenlochy Sdg.
Sdg. to Goods Stn.
FORT WILLIAM
ROUTE MILEAGE
Mallaig Jc.
Banavie Jc.
BANAVIE
CORPACH
LOCHEILSIDE
GLENFINNAN
ROUTE MILEAGE
LOCHAILORT
BEASDALE
ARISAIG
MORAR
MALLAIG
ROUTE MILEAGE

last miles. The special difficulty of working the Mallaig section in steam days is featured in the journey logs in Chapter 4.

The gradient profile itself reveals, or at least implies, a good deal about the problems inherent in building the West Highland Line — working at high altitude, the need for many viaducts and the requirement for the consolidation of trackbed foundations over boggy moorland areas. It implies also a remote and sparsely-populated region ill-suited for the establishment and support of a huge labour force and the transport of a vast quantity of construction materials. All these were indeed serious problems for the engineers and contractors. It is true that some of the transport difficulties were eased by the use of water transport on the lochs in the southern and northern stretches and also the use of the existing Oban Line in Strathfillan.

Not all the problems were caused solely by the topography as such. In principle, the builders of the West Highland Line should have been able to benefit from the wealth of experience in the construction of railways in remote, mountainous regions both in Britain and abroad to a greater extent than they in fact did. The overriding problem was that the financial resources of the West Highland Railway Company were so slender and this dictated the adoption of the least costly solutions. It was such a different story when the Midland Railway had set out, some 20 years previously, to construct the Settle & Carlisle Railway.

*Above left:*
**The southern section of the West Highland has its share of rugged scenery. Class 27 No D5382 approaches Ardlui from Glen Falloch with an up freight on 28 April 1971.** *J. H. Cooper-Smith*

*Top right:*
**The Tyndrum 'Horseshoe' is one of the most dramatic stretches of the line. This heavy summer season train from Fort William seen crossing the five-span southern viaduct in about 1948 was hauled by 'Glen' 4-4-0 No 62497 *Glen Mallie*, piloted by 'K2' 2-6-0 No 61786.** *B. V. Franey*

*Above right:*
**Class 37 No 37022 heads an up freight across the nine-span northern viaduct on 14 July 1981.** *M. M. Hughes*

The Midland had great resources, though even these were strained by the huge costs involved, and the course of the line across the Pennines was eased by extensive earthworks and tunnelling. In all, 14 tunnels with a total length of 3½ miles were built. By contrast, the West Highland Railway on its way to Fort William had one tunnel only — the miniscule rock tunnel of 47yd by Loch Lomond (the 150yd tunnel by Loch Treig was not built until 1932 when the track had to be realigned to allow for the raising of the water level consequent on the Lochaber Hydro-Electric scheme).

Similar financial constraints applied during the construction of the Mallaig Extension Line in 1897-1901. In the matter of tunnelling however, it was found essential to construct the series of short tunnels between Lochailort and Arisaig to break through the 'rock wall' of the coastal area which barred the way to Mallaig (further north it was this wall which was responsible for the long delay in completing the Dingwall & Skye Railway from Strome Ferry to Kyle of Lochalsh).

The problem of trackbed foundations proved serious indeed, both on the Fort William and the Mallaig sections — at Rannoch Moor and in the Back of Keppoch area near Arisaig. After some abortive works at Rannoch, the difficulty was only overcome by going back some 60 years to the ingenious technique used by George Stephenson for crossing Chat Moss on the Liverpool & Manchester Railway — the famous 'floating rafts' of brushwood. The peat bogs of the Back of Keppoch were even more troublesome and the only answer was the expensive one of building an embankment on to the solid rock at depths of 15 to 20ft.

The West Highland Line certainly is a line of viaducts and bridges and these are the most impressive structures of the route. What they lack in length compared with say, the Settle & Carlisle's Ribblehead Viaduct, is compensated for by their generally graceful lines or dramatic settings. The viaducts of the Fort William section are as it were 'conventional' with

*Above:*
**The setting by County March Summit (1,024ft) is truly majestic with the great 'cone' of Beinn Dòrain (3,524ft) as the backcloth. The train was a SLOA Special returning from Fort William on 2 June 1985 hauled by a pair of Class 37s.**
*J. H. Cooper-Smith*

*Right:*
**The only significant tunnel between Craigendoran Junction and Fort William was not built until 1932 when the track alongside Loch Treig was realigned to allow for the much higher water level consequent on the Lochaber Hydro-Electric Scheme. Class 37 No 37188 heads the 07.00 Mallaig-Glasgow away from the southern portal of the 150yd tunnel on 21 July 1983.** *M. M. Hughes*

*Below right:*
**The awesome Monessie Gorge cut out by the River Spean. Class 37 No D6936 passes with an up freight on 8 May 1968.**
*C. W. R. Bowman*

their masonry piers and lattice girders, but those of the Mallaig Extension Line were of greater engineering interest because they were built in concrete. Pride of place must be given to Glenfinnan Viaduct — 1,248ft long with 21 concrete arches each of 50ft — set on the curve in its dramatic surroundings. The viaduct across Glen Borrodale, near Beasdale, has a main span of 127ft which today must seem a very modest affair in concrete, but it was a remarkable advance in design and engineering when it was built at the end of the

19th century. John Thomas's book describes the work of the contractors for the Mallaig Extension Line, Robert McAlpine & Sons, and how Robert McAlpine was known as 'Concrete Bob'. It is one of the happier touches in the naming of locomotives that Class 37/4 diesel No 37425 is named *Sir Robert McAlpine* on one side and *Concrete Bob* on the other! Other impressive viaducts along the line are in the southern section at Craig-en-Arden and Glen Falloch and further on at the Tyndrum 'Horseshoe Curve' and by Rannoch station.

Another structure of note is not on a grand scale — the rock cutting at Cruach, north of Rannoch, of which 205yd is roofed over to provide Britain's only Snow Shed. The swing bridge immediately west of Banavie station is small but of special interest both in relation to the Caledonian Canal and in its design. Because the canal is quite narrow, the Banavie Bridge was pivoted from a pier on the bank instead of the usual practice of using a midstream pier. One gets a good view from the bridge of the great series of locks designed originally by Thomas Telford to overcome the 90ft difference in level between the waters of Loch Eil and Loch Lochy. According to Samuel Smiles, it was Telford himself who gave the locks the splendid name of 'Neptune's Staircase'.

This summary of the course and construction of the West Highland Line could carry the implication that the railway enthusiast has eyes only for gradient boards and engineering structures and fails to see the great beauty and interest of the natural setting. This is not so at all. I know of no account of travelling over the line by a railway enthusiast which has failed to mention at least some of its scenic highlights. To try to describe all these would turn my book into another 'Lineside Companion', but the following brief description covers quite a number of the most notable scenic features.

*Above left:*
**A key point in the construction and operation of the West Highland Line — Mallaig Junction. A freight from Mallaig had just taken the tablet from the signalbox on 27 July 1955.**
*J. W. Armstrong*

*Above right:*
**Crossing the Caledonian Canal by the Banavie Swing Bridge which is pivoted from the east bank. 'B1' 4-6-0 No 61342 is in charge of the 16.50 Fort William-Mallaig on 23 May 1961.** *M. Mensing*

There is no doubt that it is the scenic attractions of the Mallaig Extension Line — particularly between Glenfinnan and Mallaig — which have attracted most attention and praise and it is a lovely setting for the railway. But those who have travelled only over these 40 miles have yet to discover the full scenic glory of the West Highland Line. The 100 miles between Craigendoran Junction and Fort William cover such a rich variety of landscapes, and taken as a whole this section has more of natural grandeur than even the setting of the Mallaig Extension Line. The Mallaig section is sometimes described as the 'Lochs Line' and the Fort William section as the 'Mountains Line' but the first 20 miles from Craigendoran Junction provide so many lovely views of the sea lochs, Gare Loch and Loch Long, as the line takes its sinuous path to Arrochar & Tarbet. Already, the mountains are nearby and Ben Lomond (on the right, 3,192ft) is by no means the only notable feature. There follows the enchanting stretch along the shore of Loch Lomond up to Ardlui at the narrow head of Lomond, with Ben Vorlich (on the left, 3,088ft) and Beinn a Choin (on the right, 2,524ft) outstanding.

North from Ardlui, the scene becomes even more dramatic as the line threads along Glen Falloch to reach Crianlarich. This stretch is as fine as any on the West Highland Line with the peaks of Ben Lui (on the left, 3,708ft) and Ben More (on the right, 3,825ft). There is just time now at Crianlarich station to take in its commanding view over Strathfillan to the massed peaks of 3,000ft and more to the north. Crossing over to the northern side of Strathfillan, the line runs high up on the flank of Ben Challum towards Tyndrum

*Right:*
**The Glenfinnan Viaduct of 21 concrete arches set on its pronounced curve deserves to be the most photographed structure of the West Highland Line. The 13.00 Mallaig-Glasgow, with six vans included in the formation, is headed by a pair of 'K2' 2-6-0s around 1950.**
*C. L. Whitaker*

*Left:*
**The beautiful and romantic setting of the Mallaig section by the head of Loch nan Uamh. It was here that on 19 July 1745 Prince Charles Stuart landed from the French frigate *Doutelle*. The 13.00 Mallaig-Glasgow crosses the concrete viaduct, headed by Class 27 No 27004 on 20 May 1976.** *G. A. Watt*

*Below:*
**The 'Narrows' of the exit from Mallaig station frame 'K2' 2-6-0 No 61784 as it leaves with a Fort William train in August 1960.** *S. C. Crook*

*Bottom:*
**This photograph captures brilliantly the nature of the rocky coast close to Mallaig. Class 27 No 27009 approaches the terminus with the 12.55 from Fort William on 26 May 1980.** *Peter Harris*

with fine views of Ben Lui to the south. Beyond Tyndrum, there is another of the grand spectacles of the line — the sweep of the famous Horseshoe Curve between Beinn Odhar (2,948ft) and the beautiful 'coned' Beinn Dòrain (3,524ft). One may not be lucky enough to see these summits clearly but there is still wild beauty in the setting of the Horseshoe as the mists swirl down the mountain sides.

It is after leaving Bridge of Orchy that the West Highland Line enters on the wildest setting of all as it strikes northeastwards from Loch Tulla towards Rannoch. There is a special fascination about this long stretch across Rannoch Moor — something compounded of the sense of isolation, of wild beauty and of brooding mystery.

Having entered Perthshire from Argyle near Gorton, the line crosses into Inverness-shire shortly after Rannoch. The final climb to Corrour is over another great expanse of high moorland. Over the top, there comes the exciting descent to Tulloch alongside Loch Treig, followed by the swing westwards through Monessie Gorge and by the River Spean on to Spean Bridge. From there, the course turns southwestwards to reach Mallaig Junction and Fort William with Ben Nevis towering in the background. But the best views of the 4,406ft peak are gained from the Mallaig Extension Line by Banavie and Corpach. At Fort William, we are back again by the sea — the old station there had more splendid views over Loch Linnhe to Ardgour.

Where the Mallaig section scores heavily of course is in the seascapes after leaving Lochailort and in the unique associations and appeal of the setting — above all in the drama and tragedy for the Highlands of the 'Forty-Five'. The Glenfinnan Monument at the head of Loch Shiel is too poignant to be diminished by lack of architectural distinction and it is at its most powerful when seen from high above as the train crosses the viaduct. By Loch nan Uamh, one sees the point at which Prince Charles Stuart landed in July 1745. The final stretch to Mallaig gives splendid vistas across to the island chain over blue waters (they can be leaden also!) — Muck, Eigg, Rhum and Skye itself. Winter too offers a dramatic view with the snowy Cuillins and waves and spray over the line as it reaches Mallaig.

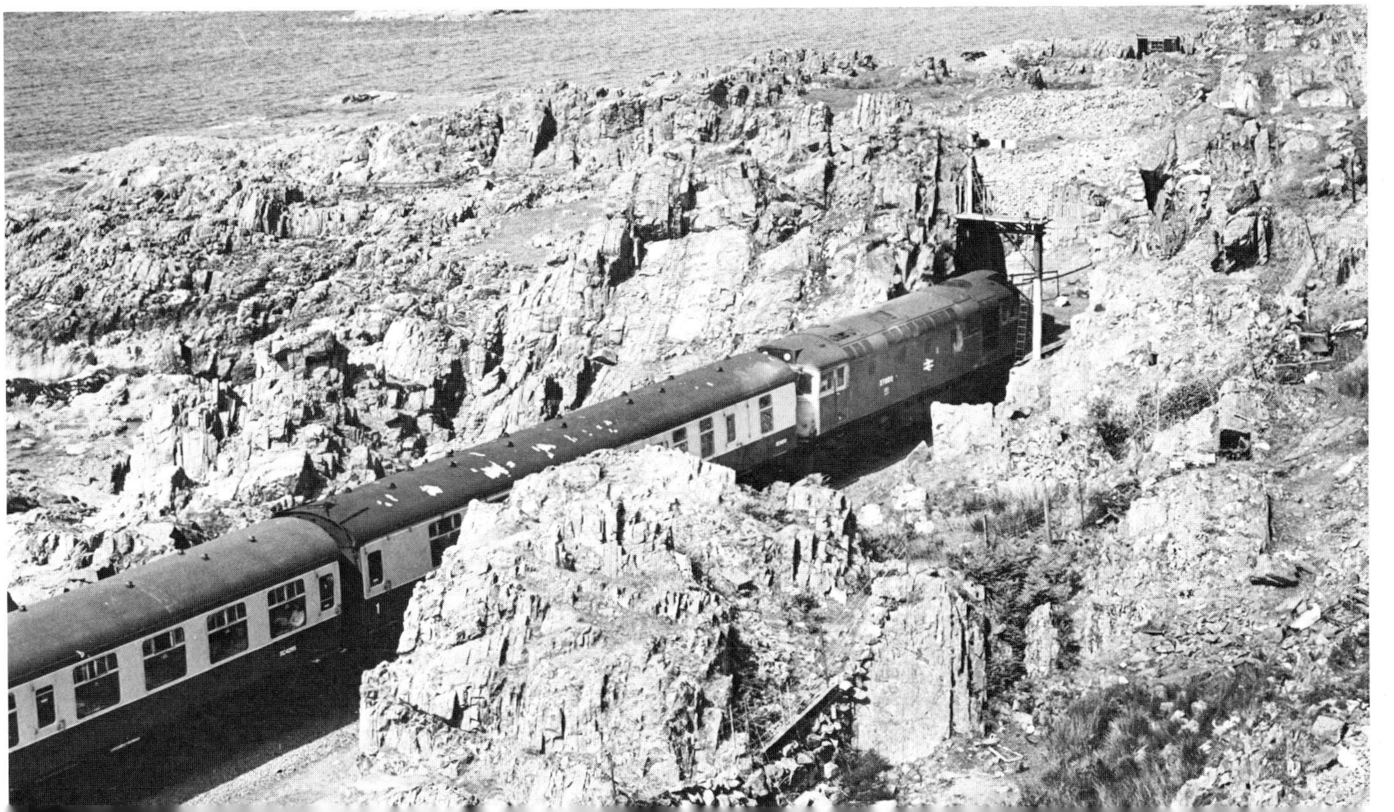

## CHAPTER 3

# The Oban Line at Work

The current passenger service provides three trains in each direction between Glasgow and Oban over the 'new' route from Queen Street station to Crianlarich and the spur connection with the historic Callander & Oban Line. Freight operations are minimal. But time was when the Oban Line was far busier than the West Highland Line and enjoyed a much better passenger service. Oban was an established holiday centre well before the railway reached the little fishing village of Mallaig, and Oban itself had an important fishing fleet.

After the traumatic years of the construction of the Oban Line, the Caledonian Railway, as its operator, put a considerable effort into promoting traffic over it. The service provided through carriages for travellers setting out from Edinburgh as well as Glasgow and there was a sleeping car service to Oban from London Euston. The Caledonian recognised the special scenic attractions by introducing an Observation Car on the Oban Line in the summer of 1914 — this was the adapted Pullman Car named *Maid of Morvern* (after the 1914-18 war, it returned to the line and continued to run until 1937). For most of the Caledonian era, the passenger coaches provided a high standard of comfort.

The importance of Oban, both as a seaside resort and as a tourist centre for the West Highlands and the Hebrides, with its excellent steamer services, was fully reflected in the summer service of 1914. In addition to six trains in each direction

*Above:*
**Stanier '5' 4-6-0 No 45356 enters Callander with the 09.30 Oban-Glasgow on 19 July 1961. This shows the delightful setting of the station.** *J. S. Whiteley*

*Left:*
**The scene at Balquhidder on Saturday 25 May 1957 when a special excursion for amateur photographers was run from Glasgow to Killin for Loch Tay. The train was hauled by a pair of Stanier '5' 4-6-0s with No 45084 leading. Balquhidder was laid out generously as a junction station but it had lost this status with closure of the branch from Lochearnhead in October 1951.** *BR*

*Above left:*
**Going well between Strathyre and Kingshouse in April 1955 is Stanier '5' 4-6-0 No 44786 with the 17.15 Glasgow-Oban.** *W. J. V. Anderson*

*Above:*
**Killin Junction on 7 April 1952 with a down freight headed by Stanier '5' 4-6-0 No 45124. The station board had not then been changed to reflect the closure in 1939 of the short section of line between Killin and Loch Tay.** *W. J. V. Anderson*

*Left:*
**The Class 27 diesels had taken over the Oban Line working when this photograph was taken in June 1965. An Oban-Glasgow train is seen leaving Killin Junction in the grand setting dominated by Ben More.** *W. J. V. Anderson*

between Glasgow and Oban, there were sleeping car trains to and from London Euston. The early morning train from Oban at 07.30 was a 'Corridor Express' through to Euston. It must be admitted that journey times over the line were long. The best time for the 71 miles from Oban to Callander was 150min for the 15.00 train, giving an overall average speed of no more than 28mph. But over such a taxing course, and with some 10 stops en route, there was a good deal of hard work involved in keeping good time. The 117-mile journey to Glasgow took about 4hr 20min.

Even in the 1920s, the Oban Line continued to be quite well served for its large holiday and tourist traffic, and was the destination for a considerable number of excursion trains from Central Scotland. Unlike the West Highland Line, however, no significant new industry was attracted to generate freight traffic and the effects of the economic depression were felt also by the Oban Line.

*Right:*
**An especially interesting record photograph of the Oban Line because it was taken on 23 May 1949 to mark the inaugural run of the 09.30 to Oban from Glasgow's Queen Street, instead of Buchanan Street, station. At Crianlarich Upper the train regained the Oban Line via the spur connection — it is seen here at Crianlarich (East) Junction. The train was hauled by 'B1' 4-6-0 No 61344.** *BR*

*Right:*
**The familiar sight of tablet exchange along the single-tracked West Highland Lines. The 09.30 Oban-Glasgow arrives at Loch Awe on 23 June 1961 headed by Stanier '5' 4-6-0 No 45158 *Glasgow Yeomanry* which was one of the very few named 'Black Fives'.** *Author*

*Below right:*
**In the Pass of Brander, Stanier '5' 4-6-0 No 45357 was in charge of an up freight on 13 May 1958.** *I. S. Pearsall*

The repercussions of the changes brought about by the 1939-45 war and by the rise of motor transport were marked and by the latter 1950s the passenger service compared most unfavourably with that of 1914. In 1957, there were only three trains in each direction, with through carriages from Glasgow and Edinburgh, and for most of the year the sleeping car service was limited to a down train on Fridays and an up train on Mondays. There was little change in journey times over the line and the best time was a shade longer than the best time of 1914.

It was hardly a surprise when the Beeching Report in 1963 proposed a radical change in the operation of the Oban Line by closure of its eastern section between Crianlarich Lower and Dunblane. There had already been regular workings of trains from Glasgow Queen Street over the West Highland Line to Crianlarich Upper, including excursion trains of DMUs for both Oban and Fort William. The costs of working and maintaining the original route through Glen Ogle were heavy and it was logical to make fuller use of the southern section of the West Highland Line proper. This section of the original Callander & Oban Line was closed in 1965 (along with the branch line from Connel Ferry to Ballachulish — see Chapter 7). It was a sad end to the story of the Callander & Oban which had served the community so well for so long.

The current service (outside the summer season) also provides three trains in each direction. In accordance with ScotRail's excellent practice of operating trains at convenient regular intervals, the departures from Glasgow are at 08.30, 12.20 and 18.20 — from Oban, at 08.00, 13.00 and 18.00. Direct comparison of journey times with those of the old days would be misleading with the use of this shorter route from Glasgow (16 miles less than the original Oban Line), but the 3hr journey does represent a real gain for travellers. The through carriages from Edinburgh no longer run and the sleeping car service has gone. There is, however, a Sunday train in each direction between Oban and Crianlarich in connection with the train between Glasgow and Fort William. The most recent change has brought Class 104 DMUs to the Oban Line which make possible day round trips to Oban with connection for Fort William and this service has helped to increase traffic appreciably. The reopening of Loch Awe station, in association with the noted Loch Awe Hotel, is another encouraging development. The summer of 1986 brought back the big attraction of a trip of Loch Awe from the station pier.

There has been nothing comparable on the freight side of the operation of the Oban Line. The Oban goods depot has been closed and the only regular movement of freight over the line is of timber from Taynuilt and of oil tankers for the coastal depots, including marine fuel.

*Below:*
**The 12.05 Oban-Glasgow/Edinburgh, hauled by Stanier '5' 4-6-0s Nos 45043 and 45162, approaches Connel Ferry on 18 May 1961.** *M. Mensing*

**'C15' 4-4-2T No 67474 heads a three-coach local working between Whistlefield and Garelochhead on a fine day in May 1957.**
*N. Spinks/Colour-Rail (SC161)*

## CHAPTER 4

# The West Highland Line at Work

For people living in the West Highlands, the line has been a railway of great importance — their 'lifeline' to the outside world. In the broader setting of railway operation, however, the West Highland Line has always been a rather modest undertaking, both for passenger and freight traffic. Happily, the experience of the West Highland over the years has been markedly different from that of most other subsidiary lines because traffic *increased* long after it was opened.

The North British Railway had no illusions about its limited revenue potential even after the line had reached Mallaig to share in the transport of fish and in the Hebridean traffic. As noted above, steamer services had developed along the West Coast long before the railways were built to Oban and Mallaig. Sea transport remained fully competitive for the movement of bulky goods and a substantial amount of merchandise traffic could benefit little from the quicker delivery over the West Highland Line. Nor was there in those times a container system to reduce the costs of the transfer of freight between railway and ship. The freight traffic over the line during its first 25 years or so was limited indeed.

Local passenger traffic was bound to be light in what was one of the most thinly-populated regions of Great Britain. The tourist traffic certainly developed appreciably but this was important only during the short summer season. In such a situation the passenger services between Glasgow, Fort William and Mallaig were always light. The summer service in 1914 provided three trains in each direction between Glasgow and Mallaig:

*Above left:*
**Reid's 4-4-2T of 1911, LNER Class C15, gave long and excellent service working the local trains to Arrochar & Tarbet (and also the Fort Augustus branch). Here the recently overhauled No 67460 (push-and-pull fitted) is seen arriving at Craigendoran with a train for Arrochar in September 1957.** *C. Lawson Kerr*

*Left:*
**With the tablet at the ready, Stanier '5' 4-6-0 No 44973 arrives at Arrochar & Tarbet with an up freight on 15 July 1955.** *W. A. Camwell*

*Above:*
**Seen climbing from Arrochar & Tarbet to Glen Douglas on 16 August 1951, No 61722 was one of the 'K2/1' Moguls introduced in 1931 as rebuilds of the small-boilered class introduced in 1912. No 61722 was fitted with a side-window cab like the far more familiar Gresley 'K2/2' engines when these were allocated to work in Scotland.** *I. S. Pearsall*

| July 1914 | | | | |
|---|---|---|---|---|
| Down | | | | |
| Glasgow Queen Street | *dep:* | 05.50 | 07.15 | 11.45 |
| Fort William | *arr:* | 09.40 | 11.50 | 16.20 |
| | *dep:* | 09.50 | 12.01 | 17.10 |
| Mallaig | *arr:* | 11.30 | 13.40 | 18.55 |
| *Total journey time:* | | 5hr 40min | 6hr 25min | 7hr 10min |
| Up | | | | |
| Mallaig | *dep:* | 06.50 | 13.45 | 15.10 |
| Fort William | *arr:* | 08.18 | 15.26 | 16.50 |
| | *dep:* | 08.30 | 15.42 | 17.05 |
| Glasgow Queen Street | *arr:* | 12.40 | 20.05 | 21.18 |
| *Total journey time:* | | 5hr 50min | 6hr 20min | 6hr 8min |

These overall times for the journey of 164 miles would seem dreadfully protracted to anyone unfamiliar with the exceptionally difficult nature of the West Highland Line and unaware of the very large number of intermediate stations. Indeed, the pattern of stops made by these trains indicates something of the special character of the route as the only effective link with the outside world by land for so many years. Most of the trains made at least 23 stops en route to Mallaig for stations then shown in the public timetables.

At the southern end of the line, there was one train in each direction between Glasgow and Crianlarich Upper, together with the 'local' service between Glasgow and Garelochhead or Arrochar & Tarbet (the latter service was operated from the Low Level station at Glasgow Queen Street). At the northern end, there was a limited 'local' service between Fort William and Mallaig. The other local trains from Fort William provided connections with the Caledonian Canal steamer service at Banavie Pier and with the Fort Augustus branch — these are noted in Chapter 7. There were no Sunday trains over the West Highland Line. Opinion in the West Highlands was even more strongly hostile to 'Sabbath travelling' than in other parts of Scotland. The North British Railway was at this time operating a limited Sunday service over part of the Waverley Route between Edinburgh and Hawick, but the company was well aware of the difference between the more relaxed outlook of most people in the Borders and the stern outlook of people in the West Highlands.

The important aspect of locomotive performance is considered below but it should be emphasised now that the work involved in hauling the through trains over the route was as hard as any in Great Britain. Train loads certainly were light but the 'Glen' class 4-4-0s then handling them were quite small locomotives. The severity of the grades and the tortuous course of the line made it a much tougher proposition than say, the Glasgow & South Western Railway's Nithsdale Line where very determined and fast downhill running was the established practice.

Following the special circumstances of the 1914-18 war, the pattern of work of the West Highland Line continued much as it had been since the 1890s. The coming of the London & North Eastern Railway in 1923, in place of the North British, was slow to make a large impact on the scene. But dramatic changes were about to occur. The line acquired its first major industrial undertaking with the decision by British Aluminium to build a smelter at Fort William. From 1925, the line was carrying construction materials and supplies on a vast scale — by its own standards. The aluminium project depended of course on a major new supply of electricity, and the great Lochaber Hydro-Electric scheme was put in hand to meet this need. The substantial labour force at work on these projects led to a large increase in passenger traffic also, but it was the freight traffic which endured after the end of the construction works, including the transport of alumina from Fife.

This industrial development was all the more important for the West Highland Line because British industrial activity was declining as the economy slid into the 'Great Depression'. Central Scotland was particularly hard-hit with the rapid decline in its traditional heavy industries based on coal and steel. The repercussions on the railways were serious. A considerable number of lines lost their passenger services or were closed altogether. But for the aluminium industry, it is more than likely that there would have been strong pressure for some curtailment of the West Highland Line.

*Above:*
**In May 1959 'D34' 4-4-0s Nos 62496 *Glen Loy* and 62471 *Glen Falloch* have steam to spare as they prepare to leave Ardlui with a sleeper working for Fort William.**
*E. S. Russell/Colour-Rail (SC163)*

*Below:*
**With safety valves lifting, 'K4' 2-6-0 No 61995 *Cameron of Lochiel* takes water at Crianlarich Upper station in June 1960 prior to departing with an up special working. Note the two Gresley vehicles immediately behind the locomotive.**
*F. Hornby/Colour-Rail (SC79)*

*Top:*
**In April 1961 'K1/1' 2-6-0 No 61997 *MacCailin Mor* approaches Glenfinnan with a down freight.**
*D. M. C. Hepburne-Scott/Colour-Rail (SC401)*

*Above:*
**'K1' 2-6-0 No 62052 waits to leave Mallaig with a train for Fort William in June 1961.**
*D. H. Beecroft/Colour-Rail (SC548)*

## Locomotive Performance in the 1930s

It would be difficult to appreciate fully the splendid work of locomotives and their crews without looking at a few at least of the logs compiled during the 1930s. These are not as rare as John Thomas supposed and, with Oswald Nock's kind permission, I have selected some of his logs from 1934. When Cecil J. Allen drew attention to these, he remarked:

'Over the fearsome grades of the West Highland Line spectacular running is hardly to be expected; but the steady work of the North British "Glen" 4-4-0s and Gresley two-cylinder 2-6-0s up these lengthy and formidable climbs is worthy of some publicity, especially in view of the

*Top:*
**On the up journey, the climb to Glen Douglas (564ft) from the restart at Arrochar & Tarbet involves 5 miles at about 1 in 55. This was a big challenge for 'Glen' 4-4-0s, LNER Nos 9242 *Glen Mamie* and 9281 *Glen Murran*, seen working a heavy wartime train in June 1943.**
*C. Lawson Kerr*

*Above and left:*
**Apart from Fort William, Crianlarich Upper was by far the most important intermediate station along the West Highland Line. (Above) An up train restarts from the station on 18 June 1960, headed by Standard '5' 4-6-0 No 73105 piloting 'B1' 4-6-0 No 61355, while (Left) the 07.45 Mallaig-Glasgow arrives on 23 June 1961 headed by Stanier '5' 4-6-0 No 44957. On the left is the spur connection with the Oban Line.** *R. M. Casserley/Author*

*Above:*
**As a nine-coach summer Saturday formation, the 10.15 Glasgow-Fort William was double-headed on 13 August 1960. 'BI' 4-6-0 No 61396 piloted by Standard '5' 4-6-0 No 73077 pulls away from Bridge of Orchy.** *G. W. Morrison*

fact that the timings of the best trains are decidedly better than those of other lines of similar grading in the Highlands.'

The 'Glen' 4-4-0s had been the mainstay of the line for some 20 years. Gresley's Mogul had been designed for the Great Northern Railway in 1914 and it was introduced to the West Highland Line to ease the problem of double-heading at the start of the 1930s. These classes are looked at more closely in Chapter 5 — here the focus is on the runs themselves. **Table 1** sets out the run of a heavy excursion train from Glasgow to Fort William headed by a pair of 'Glens' — LNER Nos 9035 *Glen Gloy* and 9221 *Glen Orchy*. The load was 341 tons tare and 365 gross and thus close to the maximum rostered loading as the limit for the 'Glen' was 180 tons tare. Calls were made at Garelochhead, Arrochar & Tarbet, Crianlarich Upper, Rannoch, Corrour, Fersit, Tulloch, Roy Bridge and Spean Bridge (Fersit, by Loch Treig, was a temporary station opened to serve the construction of the Lochaber power scheme — it was closed from 1 January 1935).

**Table 1: Helensburgh-Fort William**
Locomotives: 4-4-0s Nos 9035 *Glen Gloy* and 9221 *Glen Orchy*.
Load (tons): 341 tare/365 gross.

| *Distance* | | *Times* | | *Speeds* |
|---|---|---|---|---|
| *miles* | | *min* | *sec* | *mph* |
| 0.0 | Upper Helensburgh | 0 | 00 | — |
| 6.9 | Garelochhead | 12 | 05 | — |
| 1.3 | Whistlefield | 5 | 05 | 23 |
| 6.2 | Glen Douglas | 14 | 58 | 37½ |
| 10.6 | Arrochar | 21 | 51 | — |
| 8.0 | Ardlui | 12 | 30 | — |
| 8.4 | MP28 | 13 | 24 | 35 |
| 15.4 | MP35 | 27 | 55 | 26 |
| 16.7 | Crianlarich | 30 | 35 | — |
| 0.7 | MP37 | 1 | 48 | — |
| 5.0 | Tyndrum | 11 | 17 | 26 |
| 6.7 | MP43 | 15 | 05 | 28¼ |
| 12.5 | Bridge of Orchy | 23 | 06 | — |
| 15.7 | MP52 | 26 | 55 | 42½ |
| 21.2 | Gortan | 38 | 53 | 27 |
| 28.1 | Rannoch | 48 | 00 | — |
| 1.6 | MP66 | 4 | 52 | 21 |
| 7.3 | Corrour | 14 | 17 | 46 |
| 8.5 | Fersit | 14 | 12 | — |
| 1.2 | Tulloch | 3 | 25 | — |
| 5.7 | Roy Bridge | 9 | 57 | — |
| 3.0 | Spean Bridge | 6 | 00 | — |
| 8.5 | Mallaig Junction | 11 | 35 | 59 |
| 9.5 | Fort William | 14 | 05 | — |

Although it was summer, the climb to Glen Douglas was made in 'thick driving mist' with slippery rail conditions and the 'Glens' did well to run the 6.2 miles from Garelochhead in just under 15min. They held to an average of 27mph beyond Crianlarich to milepost 43. With the call at Rannoch, it was hard going to haul 365 tons over the 1½ miles at 1 in 53 and speed was down to a minimum of 21mph at milepost 66. The 5 miles of more undulating line to milepost 71 were run well at an average of 46mph. Once over the summit at Corrour, speed could rise appreciably though subject always to the constraint of severe curvature — the highest speed attained was 59mph by Mallaig Junction. Overall time for the 97¾ miles from Helensburgh Upper to Fort William was 195min as booked — Nock put the running time at 175min to give an average of 33½mph. This is a good example of the quality of the work of the 'Glens' over the difficult Fort William section.

The two runs summarised in **Table 2** are particularly helpful in bringing out the taxing character of the long, long climb from Fort William to Corrour Summit — a total distance of 28 miles at an average gradient of 1 in 110. But they show also the demands made by the short stretches at 1 in 55 climbing from Bridge of Orchy through the Tyndrum Horseshoe, and by the difficult restart out of Arrochar & Tarbet over a series of reverse curves. On the second of these runs, Driver Carr handled *Glen Gloy* splendidly to average

**Stanier 'Black Five' 4-6-0 No 44881 stands ready to take the empty stock of the 12.00 from Glasgow out of Oban in 1961, while in the background a later generation of motive power is represented by North British Type 2 No 6108.** *M. Mensing*

44881
D6108

**Table 2: Fort William-Glasgow**

| | 4-4-0 No 9494 | 4-4-0 No 9035 |
|---|---|---|
| Locomotive: | 4-4-0 No 9494 *Glen Loy* | 4-4-0 No 9035 *Glen Gloy* |
| Load (tons): | 182 tare/190 gross | 180 tare/190 gross |
| Driver: | D. Ross (Eastfield) | W. Carr (Fort William) |

| *Distance* | | *Time* | *Speed* | *Time* | *Speed* |
|---|---|---|---|---|---|
| *miles* | | *min sec* | *mph* | *min sec* | *mph* |
| 0.0 | Fort William | 0 00 | — | 0 00 | — |
| 3.4 | MP96½ | 7 15 | 23½ | 7 14 | 27¼ |
| 8.4 | MP91½ | 15 07 | 47½ | 14 29 | 53 |
| 9.5 | Spean Bridge | 16 30 | — | 15 37 | — |
| 1.4 | MP89 | 3 35 | 40 | 3 49 | 39½ |
| 4.4 | MP86 | 9 10 | 26 | 9 06 | 26 |
| 6.4 | MP84 | 12 45 | 39 | 12 45 | 37½ |
| 8.4 | MP82 | 16 37 | 26½ | 17 13 | 22 |
| 8.7 | Tulloch | 17 20 | — | 17 48 | — |
| 3.0 | MP78¾ | 7 30 | 37½ | 7 35 | 41½ |
| 6.7 | MP75 | 15 17 | 25 | 15 11 | 22½ |
| 8.7 | MP73 | 19 40 | 32½ | 19 55 | 32 |
| | | pass | 25¼ | 22 41 | 27 |
| 10.0 | Corrour | | | | |
| | | 22 25 | 54 | 23 35 | — |
| 17.3 | Rannoch | 32 45 | — | 33 18 | 62½ |
| 6.9 | Gortan | 10 15 | 53 | 10 35 | — |
| 8.7 | Bridge of Orchy | 12 00 | 60 | 21 33 | 58½ |
| 12.5 | MP45 | 19 25 | 31½ | 28 15 | 37 |
| 14.5 | MP43 | 24 00 | 25 | 32 48 | 23 |
| 16.2 | Tyndrum | 26 25 | 52 | 35 15 | — |
| 21.2 | Crianlarich | 33 30 | — | 42 25 | — |
| 16.7 | Arrochar | 30 55 | — | 28 57 | — |
| 4.4 | Glen Douglas | 11 05 | 23 | 11 46 | 20½ |
| 10.6 | Garelochhead | 20 45 | 56 | 22 28 | — |
| 19.6 | Craigendoran | 37 25 | — | 15 10 | — |
| | | | | 2 signal stops | |
| 22.5 | Glasgow (Queen Street) | 64 55 | — | 37 42 | — |

**Table 3: 12.10pm Mallaig-Fort William**
Locomotive: 'K2' 2-6-0 No 4697 *Loch Quoich*.
Load (tons): 192 tare/205 gross.
Driver: Clarkson (Mallaig)

| *Distance* | | *Time* | *Speed* |
|---|---|---|---|
| *miles* | | *min sec* | *mph* |
| 0.0 | Mallaig | 0 00 | — |
| 1.5 | MP38 | 5 20 | 24 |
| 2.8 | Morar | 7 40 | — |
| | | — | 48 |
| 7.0 | MP32½ | 14 18 | 23 |
| 7.5 | Arisaig | 15 25 | — |
| 2.0 | MP30 | 5 11 | 31½ |
| 3.4 | Beasdale | 7 55 | — |
| 1.8 | Loch Ailort | 10 10 | — |
| 1.6 | MP22¼ | 3 18 | 40 |
| | | — | |
| 6.3 | MP17½ | 12 29 | 18 |
| 9.1 | Glenfinnan | 17 55 | — |
| 6.7 | Locheilside | 11 05 | — |
| 13.4 | Corpach | 20 35 | 51 |
| 15.9 | Mallaig Junction | 26* 53 | — |
| 16.9 | Fort William | 27 10 | — |
| *Dead slow (10mph) over Banavie swing bridge | | | |

29mph over the 28 miles up to Corrour, despite calls made at Spean Bridge and Tulloch. On the descent from the summit, Driver Carr maintained 62½mph for several miles.

**Table 3** illustrates the work of the Gresley 'K2' 2-6-0s over the Mallaig Extension Line where these engines performed especially well — on this occasion it was LNER No 4697 *Loch Quoich* with 205 tons gross. To grasp properly the work by Driver Clarkson and his engine, one should look afresh at the gradient profile (see page 12) and remember its extreme curvature. As Nock himself stressed:

'It is quite impossible to work up any substantial speed to rush the 1 in 50 banks . . . The climb along Loch Eilt is, however, the worst proposition and here 50% cut-off and almost full regulator were employed; yet with a load of but 205 tons speed fell to 18mph . . . These uphill speeds are a striking testimony to the extremely difficult nature of the route.'

On another occasion, LNER No 4693 *Loch Shiel* (Driver Clarkson again) could manage no more than 13½mph at milepost 17½! But the 16.9 miles from Glenfinnan to Fort William were run at an average of 40mph.

These runs demonstrate just how misleading it would be to try to judge journey times over the West Highland Line by normal criteria. Throughout almost 70 years of steam operation, the West Highland made extreme demands on the skill and determination of engine crews. It does not require much imagination to recognise the further challenge of working such a route during the frequent spells of harsh winter weather.

Another long war transformed the scene from 1939 with the West Highland Line on 'War Service'. It became in every way a strategic railway with the establishment of a naval base at Corpach in the north and the swift construction of a remarkable new harbour at Faslane on Gare Loch in the south. The short branch to Faslane brought a huge volume of traffic over the few miles to Craigendoran Junction. As was the case in 1919 however, the end of the war in 1945 soon saw the West Highland Line returning to its traditionally modest scale of operations. The rundown at Faslane Harbour was rapid but the branch was kept open until the 1980s for the transport of scrap metal from the plant operated at Faslane by Metal Industries — the junction connection was still evident in 1987. After the war, there began a period of gradual improvement of the road system with motor transport drawing some traffic away from the railway.

Nationalisation of the railways came in 1948 but this did not result in any early dramatic changes on the West Highland Line, and the process of recovery from the aftermath of war was protracted. Things were settling down again by the latter 1950s when the pattern of the passenger service was akin to that of pre-1914, though overall journey times were slower.

In July 1914, the down sleeper was allowed only 5hr 40min but in 1957 it had 6hr 15min. Though the passenger service showed such little change, the motive power scene was very different. There were real strangers within the gate with the arrival in the early 1950s of the ex-LMS Stanier '5' 4-6-0s. The old North British classes were departing from the line they had served so well. These changes are considered in Chapter 5.

*Left:*
**June 1960 in Glen Orchy — a down freight is hauled by 'Bl' 4-6-0 No 61342.**
*Alex Coupar*

*Below left:*
**Stanier '5' 4-6-0 No 44967 waits for the road with an up freight at Rannoch on 23 June 1961 as a Glasgow-Mallaig train pulls in. The footbridge has now been demolished.** *Author*

*Bottom left:*
**The 13.05 Mallaig-Glasgow leaves Corrour around 1960 headed by 'B1' 4-6-0 No 61134 piloted by Standard '5' 4-6-0 No 73077. This picture clearly illustrates the lonely situation of Corrour station.**
*J. A. Hamilton*

*Below:*
**Standard '5' 4-6-0 No 73078 pilots a 'B1' 4-6-0 with an up train away from Tulloch in 1960 — the long hard climb up to Corrour Summit was demanding a big effort.**
*S. C. Crook*

*Above:*
**The signalbox and footbridge at Loch Awe station on 20 June 1961.** *Author*

*Below:*
**Caledonian '2P' 0-4-4T No 55207 stands at Killin with the branch train on 20 June 1961.** *Author*

*Above:*
**North British Type 2 Bo-Bo diesel electrics Nos D6103/D6134 bring the 12.00 Glasgow Buchanan St-Oban into Taynuilt station on 15 May 1961.** *M. Mensing*

*Below:*
**The crews of Stanier 'Black Five' 4-6-0s Nos 44721 and 45153 await the 'right away' from Connel Ferry with the 12.05 Oban-Glasgow in June 1956. Note the clean condition of the stock, the fine Caledonian Railway signal gantry and signalbox and the carefully tended flower bed on the platform.**
*T. J. Edgington/Colour-Rail (SC355)*

*Top:*
**June 1948 in the Monessie Gorge: 'K2' 2-6-0 No 61790 *Loch Lomond* piloting 'Glen' 4-4-0 No 62497 *Glen Mallie*. The 'Glen's' tender still carried LNER lettering six months after nationalisation.**
*B. V. Franey*

*Above:*
**Class 27 No 27008 runs an up freight along the winding stretch of the line between Roy Bridge and Tulloch on 27 May 1976.**
*Brian Morrison*

*Right:*
**The survivors from the motive power of the North British Railway were the Holmes class 0-6-0s later classified 'J36' by the LNER. Here No 65300 is seen shunting Fort William yard on 19 June 1961.** *Author*

*Left and below:*
**In the face of threatened curtailment of the West Highland Line's operations in the early 1960s, the establishment of the pulp and paper mill at Corpach was of the greatest importance for the future of the line. (Left) Delivery by rail of pulpwood logs for the mill was an essential part of the project. Class 27 (No D5409) traverses the Tyndrum Horseshoe with a train for Corpach on 2 July 1970. (Below) The dramatic setting of the Corpach Mill with snow-capped Ben Nevis in the background. Class 27 diesel No D5346 leaves Corpach with the 16.30 Fort William-Mallaig on 23 May 1972.**
*BR/J. H. Cooper-Smith*

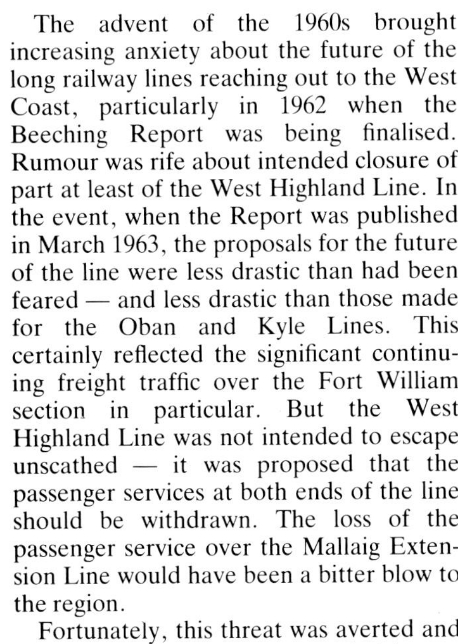

The advent of the 1960s brought increasing anxiety about the future of the long railway lines reaching out to the West Coast, particularly in 1962 when the Beeching Report was being finalised. Rumour was rife about intended closure of part at least of the West Highland Line. In the event, when the Report was published in March 1963, the proposals for the future of the line were less drastic than had been feared — and less drastic than those made for the Oban and Kyle Lines. This certainly reflected the significant continuing freight traffic over the Fort William section in particular. But the West Highland Line was not intended to escape unscathed — it was proposed that the passenger services at both ends of the line should be withdrawn. The loss of the passenger service over the Mallaig Extension Line would have been a bitter blow to the region.

Fortunately, this threat was averted and a major factor here was the decision to build a pulp plant and paper mill at Corpach with an undertaking by British Railways to keep open the West Highland Line for at least 22 years. Though the initial high hopes for the pulp plant were frustrated, the manufacture of paper has continued at Corpach with pulp being brought in by rail in part. The first major industrial plant on the West Highland, the Fort William aluminium factory, has continued to provide a substantial traffic, including the movement of alumina from Blyth. British Alcan's private siding and handling facilities have been improved recently. Other freight traffic includes the regular movement of oil products from the Grangemouth refinery to West Highland Oils at Fort William and, in the southern section, of supplies for the various important defence establishments. Now there is the new and most encouraging development of the movement of round timber from the major forests of the region. Timber is loaded at Fort William, Crianlarich, Ardlui and Arrochar & Tarbet. It is to be hoped that prospects for further growth of this traffic have been enhanced with the very recent decision by the Finnish enterprise, Kymmene-Stromberg, to set up a major pulp plant and paper mill on the Ayrshire coast by Irvine.

**Class 27 No D5363 stands at Ballachulish with a train for Connel Ferry on 15 July 1965.** *M. Mensing*

Before leaving the aspect of freight traffic on the West Highland Line, it is only right to emphasise that the operation of freight trains during the steam age made exceptionally heavy demands on train crews. The situation then was very different from that now. The lack of continuous braking called for great skill and judgement, especially in downhill running over such a tortuous line, and icy rail conditions so often aggravated the problem of handling such trains. Moreover, as the steam age drew to its close, the locomotives available for freight duties were showing the effects of the rundown of steam.

This review of the work of the West Highland has been related mainly to the years of steam operation and this finally came to an end in 1962. Between then and the early 1980s, the passenger service went

*Above left:*
**A scene in North British days around 1910. 'Intermediate' 4-4-0 No 865 pilots another 4-4-0 with a train for Fort William at Glenfinnan.** *LPC/Ian Allan Library (7727)*

*Left:*
**'K2' 2-6-0 No 61793 with the 18.30 Mallaig-Fort William near Loch Eilt on 22 June 1951.** *J. F. Aylard*

*Below:*
**This down freight seen near Lochailort in August 1960 represented a light load for 'KI' 2-6-0 No 62011, despite the taxing nature of the line.** *S. C. Crook*

through what must be called a dull patch and one cannot help feeling that some opportunities were lost for heightening interest in the line and its scenic glories. Even in the early 1980s, the traveller of 1914 would have felt quite at home with the service available in say, 1982-83 — that is, once he or she had come to terms with the diesels and the fact that the sleeper train set out for Glasgow and Fort William not from King's Cross but from Euston! As in 1914, the summer service in 1982 provided three trains in each direction between Glasgow, Fort William and Mallaig, with departures at 06.00, 08.34 and 16.34. Certainly these times were rather more convenient than those of 1914, but overall journey times were much the same. The down sleeper had a mere 2min gain over its counterpart of 1914.

Not surprisingly, it was argued with great determination by interests in the West Highlands that this service did not demonstrate positive marketing of the line. The message got through to ScotRail and changes made from October 1983 were in the right direction. The most important of these was the replacement of the 08.34 train from Glasgow by a departure at 09.50. For the first time, it became possible for people living outside the immediate vicinity of Glasgow to travel to Fort William and back the same day without having to leave home at the crack of dawn. Indeed, a round trip to Mallaig became feasible — just. The 09.50 train helped a good deal in encouraging more people to travel over the West Highland Line.

In looking at the timetable of today, it must be recognised in fairness to ScotRail that there still is such a great difference in passenger traffic between the short summer season and the rest of the year, particularly over the Mallaig section. The current service provides two trains only in each direction between Glasgow and Fort William running throughout the week — an additional train runs on Mondays, Fridays and Saturdays only. Yet again, this service would not seem strange to the traveller of 1914 — the down sleeper indeed leaves Glasgow at precisely the same time as it did in summer 1914! But the journey times as a whole do show a useful reduction on those of 1914 and there is the benefit of a regular pattern of departure times. It must be seen as remarkable, however, that the best time in 1986-87 is still 2min *more* than that of 1914.

The great change in motive power from the small 'Glen' 4-4-0s of 1914 to the Class 37/4 diesels of today should surely be reflected in a far larger reduction in journey times. It is true that the trains still have to make a great many stops en route — a minimum of 21 between Glasgow and Mallaig (rising to 23 if the optional calls are made at Locheilside and Beasdale). The main problem here is that there are now some operational difficulties which did not arise in 1914. The most important of these is the need to impose increasingly severe speed restrictions as a result of the far greater axle weights of the trains passing over what are now decidedly aged structures (a few bridges have been strengthened recently). There has also been a

*Above left:*
**A typical mixed train of the Mallaig Extension Line: 'K2' 2-6-0 No 61793 leaves Lochailort with the 07.45 Mallaig-Glasgow on 22 June 1951.** *J. F. Aylard*

*Left:*
**'K2' 2-6-0 No 61791 *Loch Laggan* heads a Fort William-Mallaig goods away from Lochailort in July 1954.** *W. J. V. Anderson*

*Above:*
**Class 27 No D5379 crosses Loch nan Uamh Viaduct with the 14.05 from Mallaig on 12 March 1974.** *J. H. Cooper-Smith*

*Above:*
**Class 27 No D5350 waits with a down freight at Arisaig on 26 September 1963.** *Author*

*Left:*
**The rail-mounted steam cranes at Mallaig deserve to be noted because they gave such long and good service on the quayside and in the yard from LNER days. Their somewhat rudimentary 'cabs' gave some protection when gales whipped spray over the tracks.** *Author*

reduction in the number of passing loops along the route.

There is one respect in which the current service differs dramatically from that in 1914 — there are *Sunday* trains. Sunday working during the summer season was introduced in 1983 between Fort William and Mallaig and now there is one train in each direction between Glasgow and Fort William.

There remains the highly important aspect of the revival of steam working on the West Highland Line since 1984. In addition to ScotRail's own scheduled summer workings over the Mallaig Extension Line, there are the charter operations of the 'Royal Scotsman' from Glasgow. These steam workings have undoubtedly proved their worth in stimulating interest in the West Highland and in attracting many more passengers to it during the summer months. ScotRail deserve full credit for these developments — it is no easy matter to organise regular workings by old steam locomotives with the limited number of crews and the minor facilities now available at Fort William and Mallaig depots. With the turntable at Mallaig removed, it is as well that the 'Beaver-tail' observation cars have disappeared from the scene, though such cars would enhance the interest of travelling over the line.

## CHAPTER 5

# Motive Power

With the similarities between the two lines in topography, construction and relatively light traffic, they also had quite a lot in common in their experience of motive power. Speed as such has never been a major consideration. The West Highland Line in particular has always had severe permanent speed restrictions. With such heavy grades and sharp curvature, the prime needs in the locomotives used have been robust construction and reliability, free steaming and good riding properties. In the latter part of the steam era it was essential also to keep down axle-loadings.

There is no doubt that the Oban Line was less demanding than the West Highland Line but it was not an easy railway to work. Its main passenger trains were generally heavier with their separate coaches for Glasgow and Edinburgh. But from the latter 1920s both lines experienced problems over limiting double-heading as trains, including the increasing number of excursion trains, became heavier.

*Below:*
**Matthew Holmes' 4-4-0 introduced in 1893 was designed specifically to work the West Highland Line and it became known as the 'West Highland Bogie'. (Below) No 696, in charge of a train made up of the special coaches built for the line, is hauled up Cowlairs Incline by cable c1900. (Bottom) No 341 was one of the final group of the 'Bogies' built in 1896 (only No 344 remained on the line by the end of 1905). She is seen at Mallaig c1903.**
*Both: Ian Allan Library*

## The West Highland Line

As the West Highland Railway Company depended on the North British Railway to work its line, it fell to Matthew Holmes to provide suitable locomotives in 1894 when the line was opened to Fort William. Holmes had succeeded Dugald Drummond as Locomotive Superintendent in 1882 and had followed the latter's adoption of the 4-4-0 type as standard for passenger working. He had already designed several highly successful 4-4-0 classes by 1893. The 4-4-0 which Holmes designed for the West Highland derived from his excellent '1890' class with some scaling-down of dimensions. It is worth noting here that nearly all the important lines of the North British had severe curvature and the key Waverley Route was also severely graded.

The 'West Highland Bogie' had 5ft 7in driving wheels, a 4ft 6¼in diameter boiler, 17sq ft grate area and a total heating surface of 1,245sq ft, with 18×24in-stroke cylinders. The engine in working order weighed 43¼ tons or 75¼ tons with tender. The first six engines were built in 1893 (Nos 693-698) with six more in 1894 (Nos 55/393-394/699-701). The class was completed with 12 more built in 1896 (Nos 702-704/227/231-232/341-346) but not all of these were intended for working the West Highland Line. The 'West Highland Bogie' was a small engine but it proved a great success with the light trains it was required to work. It ran well over the stern grades and it was thoroughly reliable in service.

By 1905, a more powerful locomotive was needed for the line and the 'Bogies' were transferred, excepting No 344 which continued to work over the Mallaig Extension Line. The first newcomers were from Holmes's rebuild during 1902-04 of Drummond's famous '476' class 4-4-0s which had performed so brilliantly on the Waverley Route and they did fine work on the West Highland. After 1907, they were well supported by several of the sturdy '882' class 4-4-0s designed by Reid — his '19in Intermediate Goods Engine'. In 1913, the West Highland Line acquired what was to prove its 'classic' locomotive with the introduction of Reid's further development of his superheated 4-4-0 'Second Intermediate' class. Though not

*Above:*
**The 'thoroughbreds' of the West Highland Line were undoubtedly Reid's 'Glen' class 4-4-0s which were introduced in 1913 and rendered long and admirable service both on the West Highland Line and elsewhere on the North British and LNER systems. No 258 *Glen Roy* (later No 62470) is seen here in pristine condition, with the North British Coat of Arms on the tender.**
*Ian Allan Library*

designed exclusively for the West Highland Line, there is no doubt that Reid had the characteristics of the line very much in mind. The 32 engines built were named after glens in the West Highlands — Reid did not share Holmes's distaste for naming locomotives. Compared with the 'West Highland Bogie' the 'Glen' was a large engine, weighing 104 tons with its tender, but it was not as large as either the 4-6-0s in use elsewhere in Scotland or Reid's own 'Atlantic' class.

The 'Glens' were a wonderful success on the West Highland Line (they also did fine work after 1920 on the Waverley Route). Nock knew their work well after World War 1 and he reserved for them one of his most glowing assessments:

'They proved ideal engines for this strenuous duty. They could be pounded up the long gradients without the slightest ill-effects; they steamed freely, and suffered no trouble from the overheating of bearings that might have been expected on so severe a route. To travel in a long train of 11 or 12 coaches hauled by a pair of them was an experience never to be forgotten.'

*Below:*
**Reid's 4-4-2Ts, later classified 'C15', were introduced in 1911 and were the mainstay of the local service at the southern end of the line as far as Arrochar & Tarbet, and also worked the Fort Augustus branch. This is an undated photograph but must have been taken after 1913 when the North British Railway adopted the practice of painting engine numbers in large figures on the tenders or tanks of most classes of locomotives.** *LPC/Ian Allan Library (0796)*

*Top:*
**Gresley's Great Northern Railway 2-6-0s of 1914 — later classified 'K2' by the LNER — provided much-needed help for the 'Glens' until he designed the 'K4' 2-6-0 in the latter 1930s. The 'K2' engines allocated for work in Scotland were fitted with side-window cabs. Only 13 of the engines were named ('Lochs') but a number of the unnamed examples also worked on the West Highland Line. No 61776 was seen at Crianlarich Upper with a Civil Engineer's saloon bound for Glasgow from Fort William on 4 October 1950.** *C. C. B. Herbert*

*Above:*
**The ultimate in West Highland motive power during the LNER era: Gresley's 'K4' 2-6-0 No 3444 *Lord of the Isles* pauses at Ardlui with a train for Fort William in the summer of 1939.** *H. C. Casserley*

The logs in Chapter 4 help to explain why the 'Glens' were the mainstay of the West Highland for some 20 years. However, by the early 1930s they were no longer young engines and trains had become heavier during the summer season. The 'Glens' had a rostered limit of 180 tons tare and this made double-heading unavoidable even where loads were no more than 200-220 tons. To have designed and built a locomotive specifically for the West Highland would have taken a good deal of time and so Gresley chose instead to make use of an existing class whose axle weights were tolerable for the line. This was his own engine of 1914 built for the Great Northern Railway — a mixed traffic 2-6-0, the LNER 'K2'. The 'K2' weighed only 3½ tons more than the 'Glen' but it was capable of hauling 220 tons tare. Fitted with side-window cab for Scottish conditions, and classified 'K2/2', 13 of these Moguls were named after lochs associated with the route (in all, 30 engines were so fitted but the others remained unnamed).

The 'K2s' brought a most welcome measure of flexibility and this reduced the extent of double-heading, particularly over the Mallaig Extension Line where they coped splendidly with the succession of short, sharp banks. Nevertheless, the 'K2' was a stopgap because it was not sufficiently powerful to haul the heavier trains between Glasgow and Fort William without assistance. Gresley's much larger 'K3', which had been introduced in 1924, had to be ruled out because of the West Highland's axle weight restrictions. In

1936, Gresley decided that a new 2-6-0 class must be designed for the line and the first of his 'K4' engines was delivered in 1937 — LNER No 3441 *Loch Long*. The total weight was kept down to 112½ tons (the 'K3' weighed over 124 tons). After No 3441 had proved itself, another five engines were put in hand and for these the long-established geographical names were displaced by names of clan chiefs. The 'K4' could haul 300 tons unaided and once again the extent of double-heading could be reduced. The one remaining problem was that axle-weight restrictions ruled out the use of the 'K4' with a pilot engine and the heaviest excursion trains had still to be operated by pairs of 'Glens' — this happened also with the running over the line of the cruise train the 'Northern Belle'.

The last development of motive power in the LNER era came in 1945 when Thompson rebuilt 'K4' No 3445 as a two-cylinder engine with a boiler pressure of 225lb/sq in. This was classified as a 'K1/1' but it retained the name *Mac Cailin Mor*, though it was some time before it returned to work on the West Highland Line. Peppercorn's modification of the 'K1/1' design, which included lengthening the engine, was not introduced until after nationalisation. A number of these 'K1' engines came to work the West Highland during the 1950s. The final decade of steam brought the eclipse of the LNER Moguls with the Thompson 'B1' and Stanier '5' 4-6-0s dominating the scene. Only a few of the BR Standard '5' 4-6-0s and '4' 2-6-0s came to work the West Highland.

The 'local' passenger trains were worked for the best part of 50 years by the North British tank engines, especially by Reid's LNER 'C15' 4-4-2Ts of 1911, and his 1915 superheated development therefrom, the LNER 'C16s' which gave stalwart service on the Glasgow to Arrochar & Tarbet trains. The 'C15s' were also used on the Fort Augustus branch where they replaced the Drummond 'R' 4-4-0Ts which had been used from 1907 when the North British began to work the line.

The West Highland Line has been one of the railways to feature 'Mixed Train' working, especially over the Mallaig Extension Line, with vans being attached to scheduled passenger trains. Most of the later locomotive classes used on passenger trains were mixed traffic types and shared in freight workings. From the start however, conventional 0-6-0 freight engines were used, beginning with Holmes's 'C' class (LNER 'J36') which had been introduced in 1888. When Reid introduced his more powerful 'B' class (LNER 'J35') in 1906, a number of these came to the line and later on some of his superheated 'S' class (LNER 'J37'). The 'J36s' saw out the end of steam on the West Highland.

The diesel age arrived in 1963. For many years, the West Highland was worked by the Type 2 Bo-Bos (later Class 27s) which had the more powerful Sulzer 1,250bhp engine. They served the line well before being replaced by the Class 37 Co-Cos with their 1,750bhp engines. The most recent arrivals are the Class 37/4s equipped with electric train heating — this has ended the ingenious expedient of using converted

*Above:*
**Old and new Moguls at Mallaig in August 1960: Standard '4' No 76001 with the 17.40 for Fort William and 'K2' No 61784 with the 18.20 for the same destination.** *S. C. Crook*

*Left:*
**A reminder that for many years the West Highland trains setting out from Glasgow depended on the assistance of the Reid 0-6-2T 'Cowlairs Banker' engines which he designed to replace cable haulage up the incline from 1909. No 859 was built in 1909 at the Hyde Park Works of the North British Locomotive Company.** *BR*

Class 25 locomotives to provide heating for the sleeping car trains — the latter being known as ETHELs (Electric Train Heating Ex-Locomotives). The Class 20 Bo-Bos share in freight duties. The DMUs made their appearance on the West Highland at the start of the 1960s with their use for excursion trips. This included the running of six-car trains over the West Highland route to Crianlarich Upper from whence three cars ran over the Oban Line and the other three on to Fort William. The DMUs can hardly be regarded as suitable for operation of the main trains over the long journey to Fort William.

The uniformity of diesel motive power is rather dull and it is understandable that those of us who knew the West Highland in the steam era should be nostalgic about the absence of smoke and steam and the deep-throated 'bark' of the engines. But it is a poor sort of railway enthusiast who cannot rejoice that the line continues in full operation and that the gain in efficiency is so great. The Class 37/4 Co-Cos can haul almost 600 tonnes without assistance!

## The Oban Line

When the Callander & Oban Line was opened through to Oban in 1880, the Caledonian's passenger locomotive classes were unsuitable for working the new railway because they had been designed for hauling heavy trains at high speed. George Brittain had become Locomotive Superintendent in 1876 and he was in post until 1882. He had intended to work the Oban Line with his large 2-4-2Ts but these were altogether unequal to the task. Instead, Brittain had to use some of the 'Heavy Minerals' — 0-4-2 engines with 5ft 2in driving wheels (from the batch built by Neilsen in the early 1870s). The 0-4-2s did good work on the steep banks but they were unsatisfactory for the sharp curvature of the route. Brittain had to design an engine specifically for the Oban Line and he decided on a 4-4-0 which was introduced in 1882. It became known as the 'Oban Bogie' and there was quite a close resemblance between it and the famous 'Skye Bogie' of the Highland Railway which also appeared in 1882. Brittain's 4-4-0 retained the 5ft 2in driving wheels of the 0-4-2 minerals engine and it had large 18in × 24in cylinders. According to Nock, the 'Oban Bogie' engines were highly successful both for passenger and freight duties and they continued in service for the next 25 years until the need for a more powerful locomotive became pressing.

*Right:*
**A scene at Oban, c1905, which features two classes of locomotives particularly associated with the Callander & Oban Line during the Caledonian era: on the left, Brittain's 'Oban Bogie' 4-4-0 No 165 and on the right, McIntosh's 4-6-0 No 54.**
*R. A. Chrystal*

*Below:*
**An interesting pairing of Caledonian Railway engines hauling a heavy summer season train and approaching Oban, shortly after the 1923 Grouping. 'Standard Goods' 0-6-0, LMS No 17424, pilots McIntosh 4-6-0, LMS No 14607.**
*H. C. Casserley*

McIntosh had become Locomotive Superintendent in 1895 and, instead of designing another 4-4-0 class for the Oban Line, he decided to build a small 4-6-0 with 5ft driving wheels. His aim was to provide an engine which would cope readily with the hard steaming up the fairly short banks of the line. The 4-6-0 appeared in 1902 with two engines, Nos 49 and 50. They proved very efficient and helped to reduce the extent of double-heading. The subsequent '55' 4-6-0s also shared in the working of the Oban Line and were still at work on it at the end of the Caledonian era. The last phase of that era brought another 4-6-0 class to the line — Pickersgill's small-boilered engine which was sometimes described as his 'Oban Bogie'. After the Grouping in 1923, some of Pickersgill's 4-4-0 engines of the '72' class introduced in 1920 put up many good performances on the Oban Line. In the 1930s, a good deal of the work was undertaken by 'strangers' because the LMS transferred to the line the 4-6-0s of the 'Clan' class, which had been designed by Cumming for the Highland

*Above:*
**Pickersgill class '72' 4-4-0 No 54501 rests at Balquhidder on 15 September 1950 after working through from Perth via the Almond Valley Line and the St Fillans-Lochearnhead link which was broken in the following year with closure of the section as far as Comrie.** *H. D. Bowtell*

*Left:*
**One of the ex-Highland Railway 'Clan' 4-6-0s which were transferred to the Oban Line in the 1930s — No 1476 *Clan Fraser* waits to leave Callander with the 13.28 to Oban on a summer's day in 1938.**
*Ian Allan Library*

Railway and built during 1919-21. They were excellent engines and Nock has recalled a run with No 14766 *Clan Chattan* hauling 10 corridor coaches up the 1 in 60 climb from Balquhidder to Glenoglehead at a steady 17-18mph. After nationalisation, the main work of the Oban Line fell to the Stanier '5' 4-6-0s and these continued right up to the end of steam operation. There were also some BR Standard '5' and Thompson 'B1' 4-6-0s — the latter had come to the line from the late 1940s with workings of trains from Glasgow over the West Highland route to Crianlarich Upper.

As far as freight operations were concerned, a good deal of the work in the 1920s and 1930s fell to the McIntosh and Pickersgill 0-6-0 classes. These continued to serve until the end of steam on the Ballachulish branch and on the mixed trains of the little Killin branch. But the locomotives which will always be particularly associated with these branches were the sturdy, good-looking 0-4-4T classes by McIntosh and Pickersgill and the post-Grouping development of McIntosh's '439' class. Towards the end of steam, Standard '4' 2-6-4T engines worked the Killin branch.

The first diesel locomotives used on the Oban Line in 1961 were the NBL Type 2 Bo-Bos (later Class 29s) working in pairs. They proved to be a short-lived class and the BRCW Class 27 Bo-Bos replaced them. Now the Class 37 Co-Cos rule the entire West Highland scene. DMU sets were used for excursion trains from 1960, and still are used between Oban and Crianlarich.

## Engine Sheds

The sheds of the West Highland Lines were few in number and small as one would expect given their light traffics. But these sheds played an important part in the operation of the two lines and the men who worked in them during the long era of steam deserve that their sheds should not be ignored here.

The Oban Line was so short, and Callander itself was so close to Stirling, that there was need for only one significant shed — that at Oban itself. Killin and Ballachulish were sub-sheds to Stirling and Oban respectively but were effectively stabling points.

The West Highland Line's sheds were at Crianlarich, Fort William and Mallaig. The Crianlarich shed was closed long ago although the building remains in use as an engineer's store. Fort William shed was close by the old station and it was a good two-road building with pleasant touches in its arched windows and large bargeboards. It was also a shed with a view, as one looked up from it to the towering flanks of Ben Nevis. The shed had a turntable of course as Fort William had been built as a terminus station. As late as the mid-1950s, Fort William had a substantial allocation which included survivors of the 'K2' and 'J36' classes together with the famous 'K1/1s'. It seemed a little odd when Fort William came under Perth as 63B, given that rail communication between Perth and Fort William was over such a roundabout route.

Mallaig's little single-road shed and its turntable have been swept away in the new layout there and this has lost us the shed with perhaps the most enthralling setting of any in Britain — with the sea almost lapping its walls and with such lovely views over the Sound of Sleat and Loch Nevis. The turntable was important for many years in the operation of the intriguing 'Beaver-tail' Observation Cars as well as for turning locomotives.

*Above:*
**Steam and diesel at Oban on 22 June 1961. Stanier '5' 4-6-0 No 45115 is in charge of the 18.00 for Glasgow while a pair of the newly-introduced NBL Type 2 diesels, Nos D6109/6110 are ready to depart with the 17.15 for the same destination.** *Author*

*Above right:*
**Fort William shed on 19 June 1961 — a grimy scene but this was unavoidably part of steam working, the end of which was close at hand. By this time, the Stanier 'Black Fives' were the mainstay of West Highland Line motive power.** *Author*

*Right:*
**Oban shed on 13 May 1961. The 0-4-4T No 55263 belonged to the more powerful class developed after Grouping from the McIntosh 'Standard Passenger' 439 class. In the background, a Stanier '5' 4-6-0 rests near the coaling stage. Note the large and small snow ploughs stored in the foreground.** *M. Mensing*

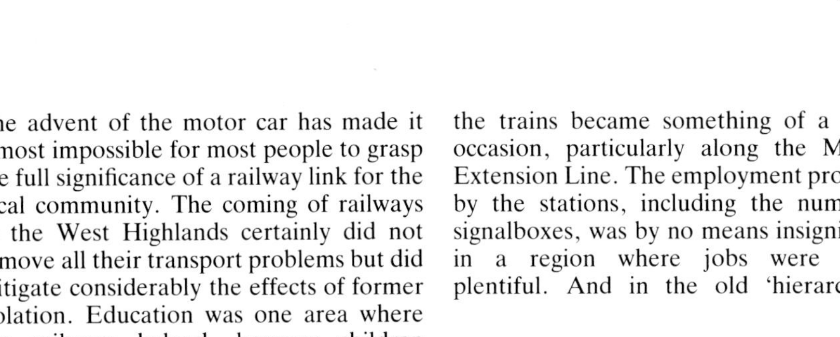

## CHAPTER 6

# Stations

The advent of the motor car has made it almost impossible for most people to grasp the full significance of a railway link for the local community. The coming of railways to the West Highlands certainly did not remove all their transport problems but did mitigate considerably the effects of former isolation. Education was one area where the railways helped, because children could be taken by train to schools which would otherwise have been too distant. Another aspect of the rail link was the excellent parcels service to the smallest of stations which was such a help to those living far from good shopping facilities.

It is not surprising that there was keen interest in and warm attachment to the local stations. The arrival and departure of the trains became something of a social occasion, particularly along the Mallaig Extension Line. The employment provided by the stations, including the numerous signalboxes, was by no means insignificant in a region where jobs were never plentiful. And in the old 'hierarchical' times, senior staff on the railways had real standing in their local communities.

Here it is possible to mention only a small proportion of the 50 or so stations of the West Highland Lines and their branches, although the illustrations convey something of their character and settings. Though there have been some significant changes since the 1960s, especially at the few large stations (large, that is, by the standards of the two lines), a good many stations remain very much as they were even before the Grouping.

The West Highland Line has always had stations in plenty with something like 25 strung out quite evenly along the 140 miles from Craigendoran Junction to Mallaig. It is necessary to state 'something like'

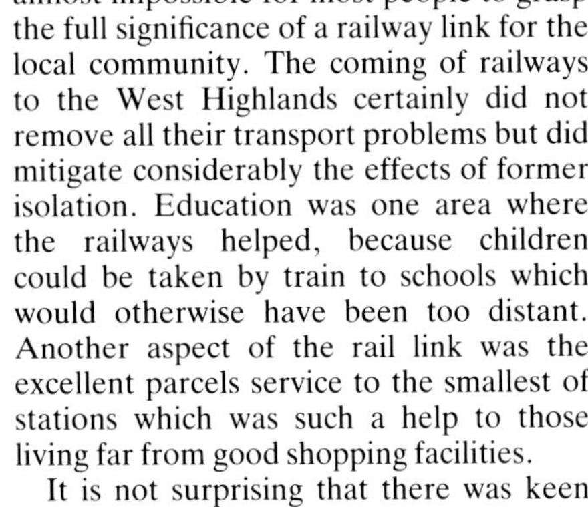

*Below:*
**A West Highland on the West Highland! The scene at Crianlarich Upper on 23 June 1961 with 'Meg' waiting patiently for the 08.30 Glasgow-Mallaig. It is apt indeed that ScotRail are now using the West Highland White Terrier as the line's logo for the Class 37/4 diesels and station signs. The 'Chalet' style of the station buildings is evident.** *Author*

because of the niceties in defining *station* with several stations opened as 'Private', their treatment in the public timetables at different periods and the matter of access to them by the public. Remarkably, there were still 23 stations open in 1987, including the 'new' station of Loch Eil Outward Bound between Corpach and Locheilside.

It would be an extravagance to claim significant architectural merit for the stations of the West Highland Line. There never was money to be lavished on station buildings, and in any case it would have been a nonsense to have built such stations with the limited traffics available and in such scenic surroundings. What can be said of them is that their general design was pleasant and not unduly abrasive in their natural setting. This design has been termed 'Chalet-style' which is fair enough given the pitch and overhang of their tiled roofs.

There was a good deal of variety in station track layouts with island, single and double platforms (latterly there have been changes here). Virtually all stations had at least a public siding and several had a dock platform for goods and livestock. The imprint of the North British Railway was everywhere in the design of the signal-boxes, water tanks and columns, station boards, lampposts and those so-distinctive tall lattice-post signals. Indeed, even in 1987, one could see plainly along the line that it was part of the North British empire.

Fort William station changed little between the 1890s and 1975 when a completely new station was built about ½-mile north of the original. This is rather 'clinical' compared with the old station and it lacks those enchanting views over Loch Linnhe from the platforms. But the old station was always difficult for train movements, and the new one is a great improvement operationally. The old station was hard by the MacBrayne Pier but the importance of the steamer service has declined.

Apart from Fort William, the West Highland Line had only two substantial stations — Mallaig and Crianlarich. Mallaig station itself has changed little apart from the removal of the platform canopies

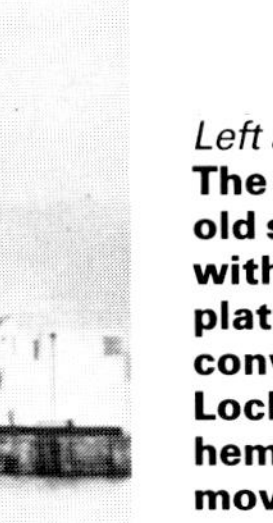

*Left and below:*
**The two faces of Fort William: (Left) The old station as it was in September 1963 with its single and island platforms and platform canopies. It was placed most conveniently for the MacBrayne Pier on Loch Linnhe (background right) but the hemmed-in site was very difficult for train movements. (Below) The station as it is now, photographed on 30 March 1987, after the relocation which has provided a much improved layout operationally, though the new station lacks the character of the former one. On the left, Class 37/4 No 37425 waits to leave with the 14.15 for Glasgow.** *Both: Author*

and the remodelled entrance hall and booking office. But the quayside track, engine shed and turntable have now all gone. Crianlarich station is little-changed and, as stated previously, the small engine shed remains in use as an engineer's store. Its private refreshment room continues to provide excellent service though not with the same lavish 'basket meals' of the old days.

Rannoch station has lost its footbridge but otherwise is much the same as ever. It has always seemed to be more substantial than one would have expected in such a setting but the 'isolation' of Rannoch has been somewhat overdone. The West Highland Railway built the road eastwards to Kinloch Rannoch which by the 1890s had become quite a tourist centre with several sizeable hotels. Kinloch Rannoch could be reached also from the Highland Railway and the Loch Rannoch Hotel was advertising in 1906 that trains would be met both at Rannoch and at Struan stations.

Spean Bridge station is little-changed from the days when it was the junction station for the Invergarry & Fort Augustus Railway. There are vivid reminders of that railway — the Booking Office stands, in use as the Post Office, and the former engine shed is intact. On the Mallaig section, Banavie was for long a charming little station with its 'chalet', flower beds and white palings but the charm has gone now with its rebuilding. Beasdale still has

*Top:*
**Banavie station as it was in September 1963. With neat flower beds, trim hedges and white palings, it was perhaps a shade 'suburban' for a setting so close to Ben Nevis, but it was a credit to the staff. The station, which has since been rebuilt, is less attractive.** *Author*

*Above:*
**Mallaig station as it was in 1963 — a well laid-out terminus of the line. The island platform remains today but the canopies have gone, along with the quayside tracks, engine shed and turntable. However, the entrance hall and booking office have been much improved.** *Author*

its park-like railings which seemed so apt for a private station (for Arisaig House) but the estate cottages by the platform are now derelict.

The Callander & Oban Line had rather more substantial stations than those of the West Highland Line. Many, including some along the Ballachulish branch as at Kentallan and Appin, had platform canopies. Callander itself was a well-laid-out junction station, as was Balquhidder, but this is history with the Oban Line closed eastwards from Crianlarich. Connel Ferry was a good example of an attractive small junction station in the days of the Ballachulish branch. There is no doubt that Loch Awe has been the most attractive small station of all with its glorious setting at the head of the great inland loch and the lovely views over the water to the ruined Kilchurn Castle. And the station garden was always charming and so well-kept.

The terminus of the line at Oban has been by far the most impressive station of all on the West Highland Lines with such a splendid overall roof. Though sited hard by the shore, it is a less restricted site than that of the old station at Fort William. Sadly, the roof has become unsafe and trains have to be worked from the double platforms outside the roofed part. Oban station had the distinction of quite sizeable trees on what was the main platform!

The illustrations here show the pride taken in keeping them attractive and in adorning so many of them with flowers and

*Top:*
**Killin Junction station was built as an exchange platform for the branch to Killin and Loch Tay which explained its lack of a road connection. The branch is seen to the left of the signalbox. On 3 April 1964, Class 27 No D5367 leaves with an up Glasgow train on the main line, while BR standard '4' 2-6-4T No 80028 shunts a brake van off its mixed train connection from Killin.** *Ian G. Holt*

*Above:*
**The gracious setting of Loch Awe station with its delightful garden, photographed in June 1961. Note the handsome platform fountain and oil lamps.** *Author*

shrubs. The absence of litter also deserves to be noted. It cannot be pretended that all the remaining stations of the two lines are now as well-kept as they were even in the 1960s, but it would be unfair to overlook the problems arising from the reduction of station staff and in some cases the withdrawal of all staff. ScotRail have certainly made improvements at a number of small stations, but they must be given a 'black mark' for the hideous shade of green in which the West Highland Line's stations were recently repainted! More staff will go, of course, when the new signalling/train control system is in being and one must wonder who will then care for these small stations? Is it altogether too fanciful to think that ScotRail might be able to enlist the help of some railway enthusiasts in caring for such stations and their gardens?

*Above:*
**The very pleasant station at Connel Ferry when it was still the junction station for the Ballachulish Branch — 'Change for Ballachulish and Kinlochleven' as the station boards announced. McIntosh 0-4-4T No 55224 waits with the 16.55 from Oban as Pickersgill 0-4-4T No 55238 approaches with the 15.57 from Ballachulish on 16 May 1960.** *M. Mensing*

*Right:*
**The impressive setting of the Oban terminus of the Callander & Oban Line by the seashore. This shows the fine overall roof and the newer platforms outside it. Sadly, in recent years the roof has become unsafe and trains are now worked from the platforms outside. Class 27 No 27044 leaves with the 12.05 to Glasgow on 17 May 1976.** *G. A. Watt*

## CHAPTER 7

# Branch Lines

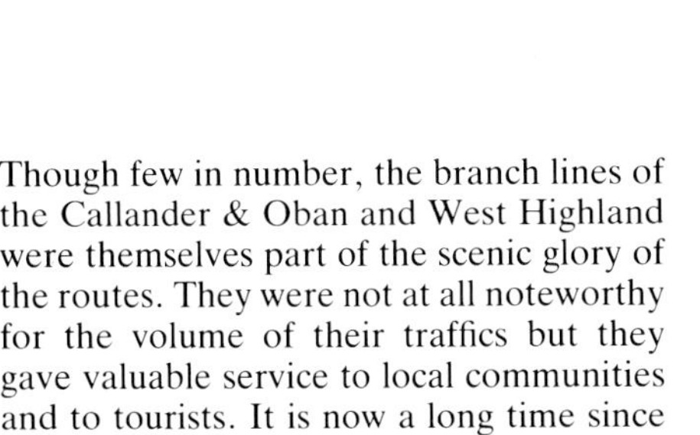

Though few in number, the branch lines of the Callander & Oban and West Highland were themselves part of the scenic glory of the routes. They were not at all noteworthy for the volume of their traffics but they gave valuable service to local communities and to tourists. It is now a long time since most of them were closed and it would be a pity if they came to be almost forgotten.

One 'branch' did briefly have a remarkable volume of traffic but it was not a branch line in the usual sense because it was built solely for the purposes of war — the Faslane Harbour link with the West Highland Line which has been noted in Chapter 4.

The locomotives used on the branch lines have been mentioned in Chapter 5.

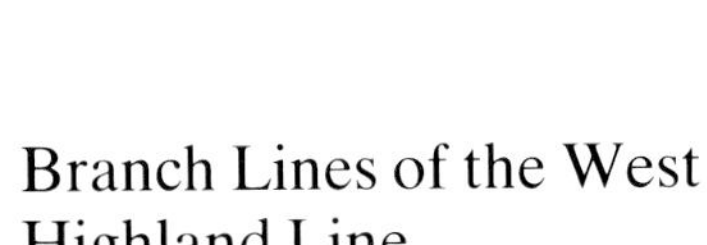

## Branch Lines of the West Highland Line

The West Highland had two branches only, excluding the Faslane link, and only one of these was built by the West Highland Railway Co. This was the miniscule branch between Banavie Junction and Banavie Pier which was opened in 1895 to provide a direct rail link between Fort William and the steamer services operating on the Caledonian Canal to Inverness. During the period up to the outbreak of war in 1914, the little branch made a helpful contribution to the tourist industry. The journey through the Great Glen was so much a part of the tourist round of the West Highlands.

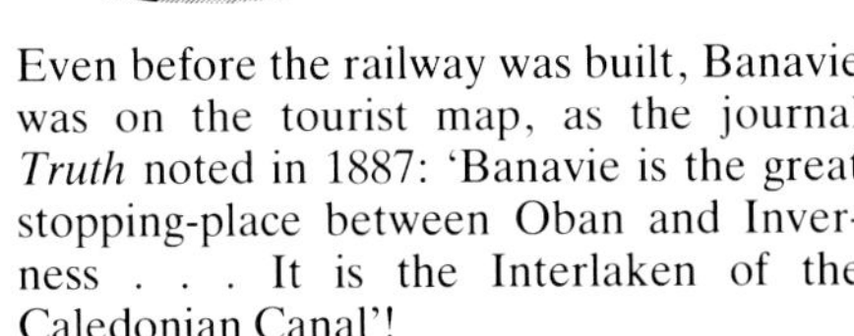

Even before the railway was built, Banavie was on the tourist map, as the journal *Truth* noted in 1887: 'Banavie is the great stopping-place between Oban and Inverness . . . It is the Interlaken of the Caledonian Canal'!

In the summer of 1914 the service from Fort William was limited to just one train in each direction and after the end of the war traffic over the Caledonian Canal declined. The canal steamer service was suspended at the outbreak of war in 1939 and the direct trains ceased to be run. The branch was closed entirely from August 1951.

The 24-mile line from Spean Bridge to Fort Augustus was the residual element of those ambitious projects for a railway to link Fort William and Inverness through the Great Glen. The small local population refused to be left without a railway despite the reluctance of the North British Railway to involve itself in a line which could never be expected to pay its way. The Invergarry & Fort Augustus Railway Co (I&FA) was formed in 1897 and the line was eventually completed in 1901. It ran northwest from Spean Bridge through the Spean river gorge before turning northwards to run by Loch Lochy to Invergarry and then alongside Loch Oich to reach Fort Augustus Town and Pier on the Caledonian Canal. It was an expensive railway to build because of the viaducts, and in addition a lot of money was spent on the stations which were far more substantial than they needed to be for the likely traffic. Because of litigation, the railway could not be brought into service until 1903.

*Above left:*
**The Killin Branch, like the Ballachulish branch (and of course the Mallaig Extension Line), saw the operation of mixed trains. On 18 August 1959 the 13.42 from Killin was seen approaching Killin Junction with an 'old stager' in charge — Drummond 'Standard Goods' 0-6-0 No 57246.** *J. C. Beckett*

*Left:*
**The McIntosh '439' class 0-4-4Ts gave good service to the Killin branch until replaced near the end of steam by the BR Standard '4' 2-6-4Ts. No 55207 is seen here with the 11.05 mixed train from Killin on a June day in 1961.** *W. J. V. Anderson*

The I&FA had been looking to the North British to operate the line, but the latter declined to do this, knowing well that it would be a loss-making operation. In the end, it was the Highland Railway which agreed to work it despite having no rail connection of its own with the I&FA. For motive power on the line the Highland used one of the 4-4-0T engines which had been built by Dubs & Co in 1893. After an unhappy 3 years, the Highland Railway pulled out and the line was closed until 1907 when the North British reluctantly

*Top:*
**The splendid twin-cantilevered rail/road viaduct over Loch Etive at Connel Ferry which carried the Ballachulish Branch. McIntosh 0-4-4T No 55208 is seen crossing with a train for Ballachulish on 14 May 1958. The viaduct remains today as a road link only.** *I. S. Pearsall*

*Above left:*
**Appin station on 29 July 1959. Note the substantial station house and the platform awning. Pickersgill 0-6-0 No 57667 is in charge of a freight for Oban** *K. Pirt*

*Left:*
**A little more than 2 years before the previous photograph was taken, Pickersgill 0-6-0 No 57667 headed the morning freight from Ballachulish alongside Loch Leven in March 1957.**
*W. J. V. Anderson*

agreed to work it. The hapless line struggled on until October 1911 when the North British withdrew. This time the service was suspended for almost 2 years until August 1913 when the North British resumed its operation. By then the Invergarry & Fort Augustus Railway was in a state of collapse and finally in August 1914 it was bought out by the North British.

The service provided over the line in summer 1914 was three trains in each direction between Spean Bridge and Fort Augustus, with one connecting train from Fort William to Spean Bridge. Traffic continued to decline after the war and the line struggled on until the passenger service was withdrawn from 1 December 1933. It was remarkable that it had lasted until then because in its last full year of operation the revenue was £179 from 1,900 passengers. The freight traffic had always been minimal and from the end of 1933 the freight 'service' was a weekly coal train run on Saturdays. The branch was closed entirely from 1 January 1947. It would not be easy to find — even in the chequered experience of railways in Britain — a more unfortunate branch line than the Invergarry & Fort Augustus.

**Branch Lines of the Callander & Oban Line**

The Oban Line also had two branches proper — the short line from Killin Junction to Killin and Loch Tay and the long line between Connel Ferry and Ballachulish. There was a third short line of 2 miles between Balquhidder and Lochearnhead which was opened in 1905, but this was not so much a branch off the Oban Line as the final extension of the branch line from Perth to Crieff which had been opened via the Almond Valley in 1867 — it had been extended to St Fillans in 1901 and to Lochearnhead in 1904. The link was severed in October 1951 when the line between Comrie and Lochearnhead was closed (the latter line along the northern shore of Loch Earn was a lovely picturesque route).

The 5-mile line from Killin Junction to Killin and the Loch Tay Pier was opened in 1886. It was built by the Killin Railway Co and though it was always worked by the Caledonian Railway, this tiny company remained distinct and independent until the Grouping in 1923 (as the schedules to the 1921 Railways Act made clear). Because of the very steep fall of ground between Glenoglehead and Loch Tay, the line was laid in with a trailing connection from the main line at Killin Junction — the descent was at 1 in 70 and it was a hard climb up from Loch Tay to the junction.

In addition to serving Killin village, the branch played its part in the tourist traffic. Before World War 1, there were three or four daily sailings from Killin Loch Tay Pier over the loch in the summer season and Loch Tay was an important tourist attraction. The 1-mile stretch from Killin to the pier was closed when war came again in 1939 and it was not reopened. The Killin branch was not closed until 1965 when the entire eastern portion of the Oban Line was closed from Crianlarich Lower.

The branch between Connel Ferry and Ballachulish was the most notable of all in the West Highlands. It was a sanguine undertaking to build 27½ miles of railway along the coast between Loch Etive and Loch Leven. By 1897 when the branch was authorised, the Caledonian Railway could hardly have been thinking in terms of carrying the line on to Fort William up the shore of Loch Linnhe. But the construction of the branch did give the Caledonian an outpost on the flank of the newly-completed West Highland Line. The growth of tourist traffic had been quite

*Below:*
**Ballachulish station's rugged setting in Glencoe with the Pap of Glencoe peeping over the top. Pickersgill 0-4-4T No 55238 waits to depart with the 15.57 for Oban on 20 May 1960.** *M. Mensing*

rapid and Glencoe was a prime attraction to visitors to the West Highlands.

It took the best part of 6 years to complete the Ballachulish branch and it was a costly line to build along such a coastline with the need to construct substantial viaducts across Loch Etive and Loch Crerar by Creagan. The Connel Viaduct is one of the most distinctive in Britain with its clear span of 500ft and twin cantilevers. The present tense is appropriate here because the Connel Viaduct was built to carry not only the railway but also a single-lane road crossing and now the entire viaduct serves road transport. The Creagan Viaduct is less striking as an engineering structure but is notable for its main spans, each of 150ft, the massive granite piers and the 'castellated' decoration at each end.

There were seven intermediate stations along the 27½-mile branch and these were well-built (see Chapter 6). The summer 1914 service was a particularly good one with five trains in each direction between Oban and Ballachulish. Even with so many calls en route, the journey time of around 105min was leisurely. In latter days, the branch service was operated between Connel Ferry and Ballachulish with connections at Connel for Oban and Glasgow.

The Ballachulish branch was truly a delightful railway with so many lovely vistas over the sea lochs and the dramatic views up Loch Leven to the peaks of Glencoe. It provided a land link between Oban and Fort William via Ballachulish Ferry — now there is the fine road viaduct across Loch Leven. It was a sad loss scenically when the branch was closed entirely in 1965 even though motorists have had the benefit of a wider road using the former trackbed.

*Right:*
**Spean Bridge was the junction station for the Invergarry & Fort Augustus Line. This shows the admirably kept station in March 1987 — little changed indeed from the early days, apart from the smart new ScotRail signs. The bay platform on the right was built by the North British for the I & FA's trains. The latter's booking office remains and is now in use as the local Post Office.** *Author*

*Below:*
**Fort Augustus station on 23 July 1931. It was laid out over-generously for the traffic likely to be available. LNER 'C15' 4-4-2T No 9155 waits with a train for Spean Bridge.**
*H. C. Casserley*